Fasting with the Lord's Prayer

FASTING WITH THE LORD'S PRAYER

Experience a Deeper and More Powerful Relationship With God

Elmer L. Towns

For more information and
special offers from Regal Books, email us at
subscribe@regalbooks.com

Published by Regal Books
From Gospel Light
Ventura, California, U.S.A.
Printed in the U.S.A.

Library of Congress Cataloging-in-Publication Data
Towns, Elmer L.
Fasting with the Lord's prayer : experience a deeper and more powerful relationship with God / Elmer L. Towns ; foreword by Jenetezen Franklin.
pages cm
Includes bibliographical references.
ISBN 978-0-8307-6880-6 (trade paper)
1. Prayer—Christianity. 2. Lord's prayer. 3. Fasting—Religious aspects—Christianity. I. Title.
BV215.T666 2013
248.4'7--dc23

Rights for publishing this book outside the U.S.A. or in non-English languages are administered by Gospel Light Worldwide, an international not-for-profit ministry. For additional information, please visit www.glww.org, email info@glww.org, or write to Gospel Light Worldwide, 1957 Eastman Avenue, Ventura, CA 93003, U.S.A.

To order copies of this book and other Regal products in bulk quantities, please contact us at 1-800-446-7735.

Dedicated to David Yonggi Cho and Jerry Falwell, Sr.

Two men changed my prayer life.
The first was Jerry Falwell, Sr., founding pastor of
Thomas Road Baptist Church, who taught me to fast in 1971.
He called the entire church and the new college we were starting—
Liberty University—to fast for one million dollars.
From that experience I learn to fast for difficult things.

In 1982, I asked Dr. Cho,
"What could I do to have more spiritual power in my ministry?"
Dr. Cho wrote, "I told Dr. Towns that I pray the rounds every day
just like a runner will jog around a track to keep in shape physically,
so praying the Lord's Prayer several times each day
will keep you in shape spiritually."

May the influence of these men
change your life as they have changed mine.

Elmer Towns

Contents

Foreword

BY JENTEZEN FRANKLIN

I believe in fasting because I've seen what happens when my congregation joins me in fasting for 21 days every January. I've seen miraculous healing in answer to prayer and fasting, and I've seen millions of dollars raised in answer to prayer and fasting. God has intervened in wonderful ways because our people have a heart for God as expressed in sacrificial fasting.

But we are not just getting things from God by fasting. We fast as a lifestyle because we know it pleases God when we meet Him in worship. Fasting is an expression of a heart of gratitude to Him.

Then there is holiness. We fast to demonstrate to God that we want to separate ourselves from the clutches and lusts of this world. Fasting and holiness go hand in hand.

I love this book by Elmer Towns. When I read one of his earlier books on fasting, I determined to get him to preach at both locations of our church in 2012. He came back again in 2013 to share more insights about fasting. As I interviewed him before our prayer meeting crowd, he pointed out an article I had written that links the Lord's Prayer with fasting. Then he told me about a book he had written called *Praying the Lord's Prayer*. I gave him permission then and there to turn my ideas into a book. He even thought of the title while we talked: *Fasting with the Lord's Prayer*. The book you hold in your hands is the result of our interview before the people of Free Chapel. I'm even more excited now than I was then about what this book can do for the larger Body of Christ.

I know that many liturgical churches pray the Lord's Prayer together each Sunday during their worship service. My hope is that this book will motivate many in that branch of Christianity to fast with the Lord's Prayer and experience the power that comes from this spiritual discipline.

I also know that many in Charismatic-Pentecostal churches fast on a regular basis but do not pray the Lord's Prayer. I hope they will experience the spiritual results that come when fasting is combined with the prayer Jesus taught His followers to pray.

As you read, notice how often Elmer mentions the presence of God. When he begins meeting with God, he always prays the Lord's Prayer. And when Elmer worships the Father through the Lord's Prayer, he experiences, in his words, "the atmospheric presence of God." I like that phrase, and I plan to use the Lord's Prayer to receive awareness of His presence.

God bless Elmer Towns for writing this book. I want all my people at Free Chapel and those who are partners with me on *Jentezen Franklin's Ministries* on TV to get a copy of this book. Read it for deeper insight into praying the Lord's Prayer, and then fast for the greatest results you have ever seen.

I recommend this book to all believers, everywhere. May God use it to bring deeper revival to His people, and may we experience more answers to prayer as we practice *Fasting with the Lord's Prayer.*

Jentezen Franklin, 2013
Pastor of Free Chapel

Introduction

When heaven is shut up and your prayers seem to bounce off the ceiling, fasting may be the one thing you can do to get answers from God. When the clock is ticking and you must have an answer, it's time to get serious and fast with your prayers. *Fasting with the Lord's Prayer* is for those who need a miracle. It is a guide for praying the words Jesus taught His followers to pray and adding fasting to your intercession. After Jesus taught His disciples the Lord's Prayer, He continued, "Now when you fast . . ." (Matt. 6:16). According to Jesus, the Lord's Prayer and fasting are meant for each other.

Fasting with the Lord's Prayer offers hope to those who continually bang on the windows of heaven but can't seem to get in. To get the most out of this book, learn about fasting and prayer in the early chapters, and then make a vow to fast and pray for 21 days. Use the checklist found on page 39 to ensure you are fasting correctly. Then sign your vow to show your sincerity to God, yourself and others. Pray the Lord's Prayer every day for 21 days and read the 21 daily devotions in Part III, which are designed to focus your attention on why you are fasting and to Whom you are praying.

As you fast and pray, may your faith be invigorated. And when your answer comes from the Father, may you shout "Hallelujah!" in thanks and praise for His loving generosity.

Part I

Getting Ready to Pray and Fast

A father's duty is to provide for his children, and a loving father will do what he can to give what is asked of him. If it's a basic need—clothes, shelter or food—a father will sacrifice to provide it for his children.

Sometimes a child wants something just to make him happy. The father may grant the request. But sometimes a child desires things that will harm him, or the request is not within the father's plan for him. He may say no. Other times, a father lets the child wait before giving what is requested. The child has to trust that his father knows best.

A child knows how to get something from her father. Sometimes she crawls into his lap and sits there for a while. Sometimes she shows her father how important her request is, or what she will do when she gets it. Sometimes she asks several times to convince him she needs the thing she requested. The father may be waiting for the right time, or waiting until the child is ready to receive what she has asked for.

A child makes her father aware of what she needs. That's a great description of prayer and fasting: God's children letting their Father know what they need. Your heavenly Father doesn't answer your prayers because you withhold food. That's legalism. Instead, fasting communicates your need to the Father, and demonstrates your trust that He will provide.

This section shows you how to pray and fast so that you—like the child who trusts his father to meet his needs at just the right time—know how to approach the Father with your requests.

1

What Is Prayer?

Several months after my first daughter was born, I tried to teach her to talk. She was the smartest, cutest and most captivating thing I had ever held in my arms. And when her mother was not around, I prompted, "Say Da-da . . ."

She smiled, giggled and flirted with me, but she didn't speak. So I kept up my instruction, "Say Da-da . . ." She continued to smile and bat her big brown eyes at me, but she didn't say what I wanted her to say. It would have been the most thrilling thing in my life if she had said my name.

Think about what your heavenly Father wants to hear from you. He wants to hear you say His name, just like an earthly father wants to hear his child say "Daddy." This simple picture shows how to begin talking to God—that is, praying. Prayer is simply talking to God. It's a conversation between you and your heavenly Father. It ought to be easy because He wants to talk with you, even more than you want to talk with Him (see John 4:23).

Suppose you are not a praying person. Suppose you're not educated in the intricacies of religious language and don't know how to begin. Start by calling His name. Begin, "My Father . . ."

The Lord's Prayer begins, "Our Father, who is in heaven." Some modern Bible teachers would invite you to say "Daddy" and some would even suggest "Papa." Whatever you call the God of heaven, relate to Him in prayer as your Father—the loving, kind, protective provider every good earthly father wants to be.

Secretaries and powerful "movers and shakers" couldn't just drop in to the Oval Office to chat with President John F. Kennedy. But when his son burst into the room, everything stopped. President Kennedy held out his arms to embrace John-John, and the most powerful man in the world listened to his dear child's requests.

Prayer introduces you to intimacy with the Father. You can burst into the throne room of heaven, where your heavenly Father is busy ruling the affairs of the universe. When you say "Father," He interrupts what He is doing, throws His arms around you and listens to your request.

Prayer reflects and enhances your relationship with God. The kinds of conversations we have with people are based on our level of relationship. When a salesperson at the department store is trying to coax you into a sale, you hold him at arm's length. When a friend talks with you over coffee, you lean in to understand what she is saying. But when your crying child comes into the room, you stop what you're doing and wrap him in your arms, murmuring words of comfort, and ready to give him whatever he needs. That child belongs to you and you belong to him, and your conversation with him reflects and enhances your unbreakable relationship. Isn't that the same with your heavenly Father?

Praying for Help

Prayer can contain the full range of human emotion. Perhaps you're in danger and all you can do is yell for your heavenly Father. That happened to the apostle Peter during a storm on the Galilean Sea. Peter saw the Lord Jesus walking on the water and called, "Lord, if it's really you, tell me to come to you by walking on water" (Matt. 14:28, *NLT*).

"Come," was Jesus' response.

Peter got out of the boat and walked on water, the first person in history to do it. But then Peter got excited, or perhaps he got scared. He took his eyes off Jesus, looked at the waves and began to sink. And he was terrified! Overcome with fear, Peter cried out, "Save me, Lord!" (Matt. 14:30, *NLT*). In other words, "Help!" If you are in danger or in a crisis today, that one word is all you need.

Praying for Healing

In the book of James we encounter another type of prayer. "Is anyone among you sick? . . . The prayer of faith will save the sick, and the Lord will raise him up" (Jas. 5:14-15, *NKJV*). If you have a critical or lingering health problem, praying in faith can make a difference. Remember the woman who heard that Jesus was in her town? She had a blood hemorrhage for 12 years and spent all her money on physicians—but she didn't get better (see Mark 5:25-26). She said to herself, "If I can just touch [Jesus'] robe, I will be healed" (Mark 5:28, *NLT*). It was admirable to want healing, but that poor woman was wrong. Jesus is not magical! He is not a rabbit's foot we can touch for good luck and long life. The Lord looks into our heart to find faith—that is where healing begins.

Jesus said, "Who touched my clothes?" (Mark 5:30). Because Jesus knew the heart of the woman, He knew that she had wrongly relied on her touch, but also that her actions began with faith. She did not have a relationship with Him—so He initiated a relationship, inviting her to come forward and talk with Him face to face. The woman was frightened. She fell at His feet and confessed what she had done. Then the Lord said to her, "Your faith has made you well. Go in peace. Your suffering is over" (Mark 5:34, *NLT*).

Notice that Jesus didn't say, "Your touch has made you well." *Faith* is the key ingredient. A prayer for God's help and healing is an expression of faith that God can help and heal. If you are sick, it's not the words you pray, or how often you pray, or even if you give money to the church (remember, the woman spent all she had to no effect). Reach out in faith and ask God for healing.

Praying to Praise

Sometimes prayer doesn't ask God for anything. Sometimes our heart is so overwhelmed with His love and goodness that we break out in praise or worship. There are so many words to describe praise. We exalt God, bless God, magnify God, worship God. What about thanksgiving? The psalms are filled with prayers of thanksgiving and with commands to give thanks. We are told, "Enter into His gates with thanksgiving" (Ps. 100:4, *KJV*) for all God has done for us. Remembering our salvation, we give thanks for eternal life. Acknowledging God's protection, we give thanks for His providence. Recognizing His guidance, we give thanks for His indwelling Holy Spirit.

We can praise God loudly in prayer and song. The psalmist says, "Make a joyful noise unto the Lord" (Ps. 100:1, *KJV*). Have you ever considered using Handel's "Hallelujah Chorus" as a prayer? "Hallelujah! Hallelujah! Hallelujah!" If you're not sure, read Revelation 19:1-6—that's a lot of hallelujahs!

We praise the Lord when we bless His name. The psalmist did it: "Bless the Lord, O my soul: and all that is within me, bless His holy name" (Ps. 103:1, *KJV*). We praise Him when we "magnify the Lord" (Ps. 34:3, *KJV*). When Mary received word that she was going to be the mother of God's Son through the virgin conception, she said, "My soul doth magnify the Lord" (Luke 1:46, *KJV*). What does this mean?

My eyesight is not perfect, so early in the morning and when there are shadows, reading is difficult. I also have problems with telephone books and newspapers—anything printed on gray. To help, I purchased "cheaters" at the dollar store. They magnify the words so I can read them. Notice: The words don't get bigger on the paper; they get bigger in my mind. Likewise, when we magnify God, He doesn't get bigger. God does not change. But He does get bigger in our minds. As we magnify Him with prayers of praise and thanksgiving, our magnifying prayers change *us*.

Praying to Intercede

Another prayer is intercession that lost people will be saved. We intercede first because we love them, but also because we are commanded to do so. Paul writes, "I urge, then, first of all, that petitions, prayers, intercession . . . be made for all people (1 Tim. 2:1). And what type of prayer is intercession? We stand between a lost person and God, pleading for their salvation. God is looking for this type of intercessor: "I sought for a man among them, that should make up the hedge, and stand in the gap before me for the land, that I should not destroy it: but I found none" (Ezek. 22:30, *KJV*). Why does God want us to be intercessors? Because He is "not willing that any should perish" (2 Pet. 3:9, *KJV*). Paul poured out his heart for lost Jews when he testified, "Brethren, my heart's desire in prayer to God for Israel is that they might be saved" (Rom. 10:1, *KJV*). We must follow his example, praying earnestly for those who are far from God.

Pray Without Ceasing

Prayer can be as simple as talking to God inwardly as you go about your daily duties. As Luke's Gospel states, "Men ought always to pray" (Luke 18:1, *KJV*). "Always" means that prayer must become as natural as breathing. Paul challenges us, "Pray without ceasing" (1 Thess. 5:17, *KJV*). But what does "without ceasing" mean? When we are at a basketball game cheering for a dunk, we're not praying. When we laugh at the comics or something funny, that's not praying. Does "pray without ceasing" mean every minute of every day of every week of every year? No. Technically, the original language gives a picture of a hacking cough or a barking dog. A more accurate translation, instead of "without ceasing," might be "intermittently." Think of modern windshield wipers. On most new cars, a sensing device speeds up or slows down the wipers as needed to keep the windshield clear. Similarly, intermittent prayer speeds up or slows down according to our needs.

We shouldn't hesitate to pray for little things. We know we should pray for big obstacles or problems that block our pathways, and Jesus said we can count on God's action in response to our faith. "If you had faith even as small as a mustard seed, you could say to this mountain, 'Move from here to there,' and it would move. Nothing would be impossible" (Matt. 17:20, *NLT*). We pray for God to remove the mountains that block our path, but most of us ignore the pebbles in the road. And that's too bad, because different situations test the strength of our faith in different and necessary ways. Mountains test the greatness of our faith; pebbles test our faith's endurance. Additionally, if we ignore humdrum problems, they may grow into huge spiritual mountains. Big things in life are made up of an inestimable number of small things, so shouldn't we pray for small things before they lead to bigger problems? Maybe you've heard it said, "The devil is in the details." The opposite is truer: "God is in the details." Let's not forget to pray about the details, and expect to find God there.

Let's also not forget regular, habitual prayer, in which we pray at a certain time and in a certain place. Jesus said, "But thou, when thou prayest, enter into thy closet, and when thou hast shut thy door, pray to thy Father which is in secret; and thy Father which seeth in secret shall reward thee openly" (Matt. 6:6, *KJV*). Almost everyone has a favorite place to pray, a place where they are most comfortable and "at home" with God. It doesn't have to be an actual clothes closet; "closet" is a symbolic word that stands for your private or quiet place. Wherever you do it, setting aside regular time to talk with and listen to the Father is its own reward. Time spent in God's presence changes us into people who reflect His character.

While a habit of private prayer is invaluable, we can pray any time, in everyday circumstances or extraordinary moments of danger. Likewise, we can pray in any place. Nehemiah, the wine-taster for the king of Persia, was in the throne room going about his duties when the king asked him a question. "So I prayed to the God of heaven" (Neh. 2:4, *KJV*), the prophet says, right then and there. We can pray at any time, in any place—and in any condition. As Jesus hung on the cross, He prayed, "Father, forgive them; for they know not what they do" (Luke 23:34, *KJV*). The Church's first martyr, Stephen, prayed as he died: "Lord, lay not this sin to their charge" (Acts 7:60, *KJV*). Whatever your condition, wherever you find yourself, you can call out to God.

Prayer Begins with Relationship

Prayer is not talking with yourself about some need. Prayer is not just thinking about your concerns. Prayer is talking with God. It's based on a relationship with God. Whether you pray in inward silence or out loud, quickly or at length, you can talk to God any time, at any place, on any topic.

If you don't know God, however, then He is not your heavenly Father and you are not His child. But that doesn't mean you can't change things and become a Christian. If you will believe that Jesus died for your sins so you don't have to be punished for them, you can become a child of God. "To all who believed [Jesus] and accepted him, he gave the right to become children of God" (John 1:12).

But what is believing? When Jesus walked on earth He asked different people to follow Him. They left what they were doing and followed Jesus. Following is believing. Will you begin following Jesus today? If so, pray the following:

Lord Jesus, thank You for dying for my sins.
I believe in You and receive You as my Savior.
I turn from my sins and will follow You.
I will live for You. Amen.

2

What Is Fasting?

When I was saved in 1950, I never fasted or even thought about fasting. Twenty-one years later, in 1971, I helped Jerry Falwell start Liberty University. When the new school needed money that first year, Dr. Falwell challenged the students and members of his church to fast for financial support. And it came. Over the years, he challenged us to fast for building projects, healings, new evangelistic outreaches. I learned firsthand that God answers when fasting is added to prayers. But I hadn't yet tried fasting for a personal need.

My wife and I were struggling to make two house payments: one in Lynchburg, Virginia, where we had moved to found Liberty, and one in Chicago, on our previous home that had not yet sold. I told my wife, "Why can't we fast for the house to sell?" The house payment in Chicago was due the fifteenth of the month, so we fasted on that date (a Yom Kippur fast, including the evening meal, breakfast and lunch). Nothing happened. A month later we did the same thing, and again nothing happened. The process went on for six months, when we finally accepted an offer.

I went to Chicago for the closing, and the buyer told me he had begun looking at my house on his wife's birthday. I didn't think anything of it until he told me his wife's birthday was six months ago on the sixteenth—the day after our first fast. The hair on the back of my neck stood up and I froze in fear. *What if we had not fasted?* Then he told me he had come back around the fifteenth of each month to look at the house, trying to make a decision. I asked myself, *What if we had not continued to fast on the fifteenth of every month?*

That first fast taught me three important lessons. First, fasting takes your prayers to a deeper level to get answers. Second, when you fast with someone else, you are agreeing together (see Matt. 18:19). And third, once you start fasting, don't quit. God may have begun to answer your prayers out of sight.

Since that time, I've made fasting a part of my Christian lifestyle. I fast for big requests as well as for small ongoing needs.

Why Fast?

Your body is a finely tuned physical engine that needs fuel to use its enormous power. That fuel is called food. To make sure your body gets the fuel it needs, God created an appetite within you to eat. Your appetite to eat is satisfied by food. God built within you an eating cycle to give you energy and keep you living.

So why would you choose to deliberately break this cycle?

Starvation is a worldwide challenge. We've all seen pictures of little children with swollen bellies and hungry children begging for something to eat with empty cups. Starving people stampede when a food truck arrives in refugee villages. People trample on one another just to get a slice of bread. While so many in the world are clamoring for food, why would you voluntarily give up eating?

Around the world, many people are glad to get one meal a day. But Americans are culturally programmed to eat three daily "square" meals. Haven't you heard "Breakfast is the most important meal of the day"? Did your mother ever tell you, "Eat so you'll grow up strong"? She also said to get some exercise to stay fit and to bundle up on cold days to stay healthy. Great advice! But that brings us to another question.

Will you be healthy if you don't eat?

Our television screens are filled with commercials for diet pills, diet programs and exercise equipment, all promising to help you develop a strong, healthy body and lose some weight. As the world glorifies and idolizes a healthy body, why would we sacrifice basic food?

Some people cut back on food to lose weight for health reasons or for the vanity of having a trim body. Is it really that outrageous to consider fasting for a spiritual purpose? Consider people with high blood pressure who stop eating fried foods and fatty desserts to save themselves from a stroke. What's wrong with a person who fasts to save herself spiritually? Just as a diabetic avoids sweets to prevent a negative insulin reaction, you may enter a partial fast to keep your walk with God your first priority.

There are many ways to sacrifice your strength. If you sacrifice your strength by working for God all day at a church outreach event, is that any different than sacrificing your strength in fasting? Not really. In both instances, God sees our sacrifice and rewards according to the faith of our hearts.

Most Christians in America do not fast. It's not part of the liturgy of high churches, and many congregational churches do not practice it. Yet Jesus assumed it as part of a healthy prayer life: "*When* you fast . . ." (Matt. 6:16, emphasis added). Why? Perhaps Jesus knew that we wouldn't get an answer to our prayers until we demonstrate our humility and sincerity by fasting. When we give up that which is enjoyable—food—we are telling God that we sincerely trust Him to answer our prayer. You demonstrate your sincerity when you give up food, which is necessary for strength and vitality. When you're willing to sacrifice by fasting, God sees your faith and answers your prayer.

There are many godly people who have never fasted and yet receive frequent answers to prayer. For example, every church has a godly grandmother who is an extremely effective intercessor. Many of those godly grandmas have never fasted. Why are they so effective in prayer? Effective intercessors live continuously close to God. While the average Christian needs to fast in order to pray effectively, the grandmother stays in God's presence and doesn't need discipline for effective intercession.

By way of illustration, imagine two men who want to keep in shape physically. One man goes to the gym every day and works out on all the equipment. His *discipline* has made him a perfect specimen of health and strength. The second man has never been to the gym and wouldn't know the first thing about using free weights or a rowing machine. But he works in construction. Every day, he slings a hammer, lifts heavy materials and climbs around on scaffolding. His *occupation* has made him a perfect specimen of health and strength.

Great intercessors are like that: occupied by prayer and God's presence on a daily basis, strong and healthy in heart and soul. But most of us are like the first man. We need the discipline of fasting to keep us spiritually fit and strong.

The Yom Kippur Fast

When should a fast begin? When should it end? In the Old Testament, we find instructions for every Jew to fast on Yom Kippur, the Day of Atonement. "On the tenth day of the seventh month of each year, you must go without eating" (Lev. 16:29, *CEV*). Those who fast for Yom Kippur refrain from eating the evening meal, breakfast and lunch.

Why does the fast begin in the evening rather than in the morning? God measures a day differently than we do: "The evening and the morning were the first day" (Gen. 1:5, *NKJV*). While we think of day as daylight, God thinks of a day as a 24-hour period that begins at the end of daylight, or the beginning of the night. The Yom Kippur fast begins at sundown, continues for 24 hours and is broken at sundown the following day at the evening meal.

A Jewish guide in Israel was asked if he kept the Yom Kippur fast. He replied, almost belligerently, "Certainly, I am a good Jew. I do not eat the evening meal, breakfast or lunch."

Then he was asked at what time he breaks his fast to eat the evening meal.

He threw his head back and laughed, whiskers bouncing on his face. "The rabbi tells us not to break our fast until we can see two stars in the sky." Then he said with a sly wink, "A hungry Jewish man may see one star that's not really there, so he must wait until he sees two." He looked to the sky and bellowed, "And I pray that Yom Kippur does not have a cloudy night!"

You may decide to wait until two stars appear in the evening sky or to eat the evening meal at whatever time it is normally served. The important point is to give your fasting day or days a full 24 hours, beginning and ending at the evening meal.

Fasting Basics

If you have never fasted, it may be scary to think about not eating—and even scarier after you start fasting. A few hours after your first skipped meal you feel hunger pangs, and nothing inspires doubt like hunger! *Maybe this wasn't such a good idea after all.* You can turn these moments of anxiety to work in your favor. When hunger pangs hit, that's a perfect reminder to pray for the request that brought you to fasting in the first place.

Some people do not attempt to fast because they believe they lack the willpower to withhold food. But the ability to stay on a fast has nothing to do with successfully avoiding food. The power to fast comes from a thirst to be in God's presence and a hunger for answered prayer. So don't try "tricks" to keep you on the fast. Some people walk around with a bottle of water to sip or a stick of gum to chew every time they think of food. If you use tricks like these, you're paying attention to the least important aspect of fasting. Focus your attention on the Lord Jesus Christ, not on the fact that you're not eating. Claim the promise, "I can do everything through Christ, who gives me strength" (Phil. 4:13, *NLT*).

Others worry that fasting could cause health problems. Many of us think of our bodies like cars: If we don't put oil in the engine, it'll burn up. A one-day fast from solid food is like driving a car with the oil warning light on. A 21-day Daniel fast (vegetables only) is like going on a cross-country road trip without enough water, oil or gas. But most people find that, rather than causing harm, fasts have a positive effect on their health. When you fast, you eliminate poisons and toxins from your body; the longer your fast, the more toxins and potential diseases are eliminated. Many who fast find their blood pressure has gone down, along with their cholesterol. (If you have a health condition that might be affected by withholding food or changing your diet, see your doctor before you begin. He or she will advise you how to avoid harming your health during your fast.)

Some people ask, "What will my friends think if I don't eat with them?" The answer is simple: You don't fast to impress your friends. Have you ever gone out to a meal with an upset stomach and ordered just a ginger ale? Other times you ordered only coffee. You didn't care what your friends thought then. When you fast, just order a beverage and don't worry what your friends think. On most occasions, you don't even need to let your friends know you are fasting. Jesus commanded His followers, "When you fast, don't make it obvious, as the hypocrites do, for they try to look pale and disheveled so people will admire them for their fasting. But when you fast, comb your hair and wash your face. Then no one will notice that you are fasting, except your Father, who knows what you do in private. And your Father, who sees everything, will reward you" (Matt. 6:16-18, *NLT*). What do these verses mean for us? God does not look at the outward activity of fasting; God looks at our heart. The outward act of fasting does not make us extra spiritual or special "people of God." More significant to God is the inward attitude that motivates our fast.

Sometimes you fast privately, not telling anyone—including your spouse. At other times, you share your fast with others and you agree together to seek a request of God. "If two of you agree here on earth concerning anything you ask, my Father in heaven will do it for you" (Matt. 18:19, *NLT*). We read in Scripture of many times when people agreed to fast together. Ezra fasted with 4,000 people when they faced a dangerous trip from Babylon back to Jerusalem (see Ezra 8:21-23). Esther asked all the Jews in Persia to fast with her for divine intervention before she went to see the king (see Esther 4:16). Shirley Dobson and Vonette Bright appeared before a House Committee in Washington, D.C., to testify for the passage of a National Day of Prayer and fasting. On the first Thursday of each May, tens of thousands of people agree in prayer to ask God's mercy and blessing on the United States, its leaders and its people.

When you fast, expect resistance. A friend may call you goofy, while others keep their negative thoughts to themselves. You may even find some "good ol' soul" who tries to talk you out of fasting. But your fast is not about them; it is between you and God. Don't break your vow, even under pressure. Satan will oppose you. He doesn't want you in the presence of God interceding for spiritual victory! He wants to destroy you and will not easily give up territory he has conquered. "Stay alert! Watch out for your great enemy, the devil. He prowls around like a roaring lion, looking for someone to devour" (1 Pet. 5:8, *NLT*).

Keep Climbing!

Fasting is not easy. It is both a physical and a spiritual challenge. It can be difficult, draining and dangerous. But it is worth the trouble! It's like climbing a mountain. Make a vow and begin climbing to your destination. Your body may say, "You can't climb any higher; you need rest." It's okay to rest, but don't break your fast in the midst of your climb. If you quit halfway through, you won't win the victory God wants to give you. If you sit down and relax for a while, that's all right. But don't start eating. Rest awhile and then start climbing again, all the way to the top.

Begin your fast with full knowledge that the path ahead may be tough. Acknowledge that you may be tempted to quit. But keep your goal in mind: the top of the mountain. When you get there, you'll see something very few people have seen.

There's a story that all young boys of a certain Native American tribe had to climb to the top of the mountain in order to become warriors, worthy to fight alongside the other men. Some young boys quit halfway up and they never attained full manhood. Other boys came back claiming they had been to the top. The chief asked each one, "What did you see?" Their answers revealed who was a worthy warrior and who was not. The chief knew which young men had been to the top when they answered, "I saw something I had never seen before. The sea."

Keep climbing. You do not climb alone—God's presence is with you every step of the way. And answers you have never seen or even imagined await you at the summit.

3
How to Begin Fasting

Before you read further, why don't you stop to pray? *Lord, help me understand fasting and what I can accomplish when I fast and pray.*

The decision to fast is like leaves on a head of lettuce. Just as there are many layers of lettuce leaves, so too there are many layers to the decision process. The first and outer leaf is a wish. Fasting is something you've thought about doing, but not very seriously. Then you hear a challenge from the pulpit or a friend or a book and think, *That would be nice* or *Perhaps I need to fast to get a specific prayer answered.* You begin to wish you could touch God through prayer and fasting. That's good. For when you do it properly, God will touch you.

The second leaf is desire. You go beyond a casual wish to a deep longing. You think about fasting two or three times a day, driving to work or during other quiet moments. When you think about spending intense, deliberate time with God, your heart hungers to begin. The more you think about fasting, the more you become convinced you could do it. You say to yourself, *I want to touch God through fasting, and I won't be satisfied until I do it.*

The third leaf is determination. You begin to tell yourself, *I know I can last through a one-day fast.* You think back to times when you skipped a meal, or even two meals in a day. The idea of fasting is no longer strange or overly intimidating—in fact, fasting has begun to sound like a very good idea indeed. The more you think about it, the more you are determined to go a whole day without eating.

The fourth leaf is planning. You might begin to write your prayer list, or to focus on your church's prayer project. You might plan to read one or two (or three) Christian books you have wanted to read for years but have never had the opportunity. You plan the place where you will pray and begin thinking through how you will manage your schedule.

The fifth leaf is something psychologists call *imprinting*. When you imprint, the decision becomes a part of you and you become a part of the decision. You have decided, *Yes, I can and will do it.* You know you can pray and get the answers you seek. You know you can touch God, and you are ready to start.

The sixth leaf is launching. This is when you actually begin your first fast. When you launch, your focus is not on missing a meal; you are looking forward to meeting with God. You retreat to your private place and begin praying. Your prayer list is there, your devotional book is ready and your heart anticipates the experience. You've prepared and are ready to meet God.

The final and inner leaf is the presence of God. When you begin fasting with the Lord's Prayer, your first petition is "Hallowed be Thy name." When you pray for God's name to be hallowed, you are crying out, "Holy! Holy! Holy!" Your prayer is an act of worship. And when you worship, God comes to receive it. Jesus said the Father is seeking worshipers who will worship in the Spirit and in truth (see John 4:23). When you fast and pray in faith, you are the kind of worshiper the Father seeks—and His presence will find you in your place of prayer and worship.

You will find there's power in the presence of God. Imagine dozens of freight cars pulled by one engine. Car after car, one after another, takes its journey toward its destination—all because of the relentless, perpetual power of the engine. Like those freight cars, you will find it easy to miss meal after meal because of the power of God's presence. You will find prayer time following prayer time because of the power of God's presence. And you will find answered prayer upon answered prayer because of the power of God's presence.

Deepen your wish into a desire to fast. Determine and plan to fast. Become imprinted with your decision and then launch your fast. The presence of God awaits you.

Lynn's Story

A junior high-age girl at Thomas Road Baptist Church in Lynchburg, Virginia, heard her pastor and church leaders talk about fasting. The church adults, as well as the students at Liberty University, had been called to fast, but children had not been included.

Lynn worked on the puppet team in the Sunday night youth group. The group was planning a gospel presentation at a local juvenile detention center, and their leaders challenged them to pray that God would use them to turn young peoples' heart to Him. The ministry team of 13, counting all the puppeteers, singers and speakers, agreed together to pray. Lynn also decided to fast.

She decided on a Yom Kippur fast (24 hours from sundown to sundown). On the afternoon she began her fast, she went straight to the kitchen for a snack when she got home from school, reminding her mother of her plan to fast beginning at sundown. She didn't eat the evening meal. Instead, she went to her room and read some passages of Scripture and a chapter in a Christian book, and then went through her puppet presentation. (Her puppet had only a minor speaking part, but she considered herself vital to the total presentation.)

The next morning, Lynn didn't eat breakfast or lunch. She had a big glass of orange juice for breakfast and then went to school. Her mother had written permission for her teacher to allow Lynn to remain at her desk during lunch period.

"It was hard," Lynn confessed. "All I could think about all day was the fact I was not eating." In her 12-year-old innocence, she confessed, "I could hardly wait until the sun went down so I could go to the kitchen and get a glass of milk and a half of a sandwich before dinner!" Then she smiled and continued, "I didn't cheat. I kept my fast the whole time."

For a 12-year-old girl to go without eating for a whole day may seem like a simple thing, but after the puppet show at the juvenile home, several boys prayed to receive Christ. Many of the students on the ministry team rejoiced that God had used them, but without telling anyone or taking credit, Lynn knew God answered their prayers because she had fasted.

Simple Preparations

If you are a newcomer to fasting, a one-day fast is the best place to start, just as it was for Lynn. You may have a pressing need or a deep thirst for God—or both—that tempt you to jump into the deep end and fast for a week or longer. But fasting is a lot like long-distance running. To run a marathon, you first must be able to run one mile. And if you haven't run one mile in a very long time (or ever!), it will take time for your body to become conditioned to the new rigors you are asking of it. And consider the likely consequences: If you start with a long fast and don't make it to the end, you may never fast again. But a successful one-day fast leads naturally to a successful three-day fast.

God is more concerned about your faith than He is about the length of your fast, or what food you give up, or other mechanical details. Giving up food is an indication of the attitude of your heart, and that is what God sees and measures.

Remember when Jesus observed people standing on the street corner making a great show of their prayers? He saw through them to the hypocrisy of their hearts. To His followers, He said, "When you pray, you shall not be like the hypocrites, for they love to pray standing in the synagogue and on the corners of the streets, that they may be seen by men. . . . When you pray, do not use vain repetitions as the heathen do, for they think that they will be heard for their many words" (Matt. 6:5,7, *NKJV*). God hears and answers your prayers not because of how long you pray, or how loud you pray, or any other physical demonstration of sincerity. It's not the outward show, but the faith of the heart that counts.

When a man proposes to a woman, it's not the length of the proposal that is important, nor the eloquence of his words. In our modern day, young men propose in sensational ways, such as climbing to the top of a mountain or skyscraper, or proposing in front of an entire football stadium. These outward extravagances create memories, but what really counts is her "Yes!" When you begin fasting, don't measure your success by the sensational things you do but by the sincerity of your heart. Your success in fasting is not measured by what you accomplish (God is the one who will accomplish your answered prayers), but by the faith that leads you to fast. Trust that God sees your full measure of faith, and start at the beginning.

Keep it simple. When the sun goes down, or perhaps a little before the sun sets, begin to withhold food *and to pray*. Fasting is not just going without food. It is a deliberate, focused way of praying. Jesus told His followers that some prayers could only be answered when accompanied by fasting (see Matt. 17:2). His assumption is that we will pray when we fast, not just skip a few meals. So pray!

At mealtime, go to your quiet place (your study, bedroom or other private location) and pray for the project for which you are fasting. A meal usually lasts anywhere from 30 to 60 minutes, but many people can't pray that long when they are just beginning to fast. Pray for a while, then read your Bible or a chapter in a devotional book that encourages you to more faith. Spend some time in worshipful meditation. Turn your thoughts to God by listening to and singing Christian music.

Follow the same sequence when you skip breakfast the following morning. Find a quiet place and spend approximately 30 minutes praying, studying the Bible and reading Christian literature. Follow the same pattern for lunchtime. If you have an office, close the door and spend that time with God. If you work outside, pray in your car or pickup truck, under a shady tree or on a walk, or in some other private place. Follow the same sequence of prayer, Bible study and Christian literature, accompanied by Christian music.

When Jerry Falwell called his church and the students at Liberty University to fast, he would announce, "Eat a small snack before you come to church on Sunday evening. We will begin fasting together during the Sunday evening service, and you'll not eat until the sun goes down on Monday. If you go out to fellowship with others after church, don't eat any solid food, just have something to drink." It was important to him that we not break our fast until the sun went down on Monday evening.

Dr. Falwell always thought Sunday night was the best time to start a fast. After all, he said, we had been in the house of God all day Sunday, nourished by His Word. I usually begin my private fasts on Monday. There is no "right" day to start. Choose a day that will work with your work, family and church schedules.

Why did Dr. Falwell tell his congregation to eat a snack on Sunday afternoon? Because there are instances in the Old Testament when God told His people to prepare for a fast by eating. For example, God called Elijah to a 40-day fast and told him, "Rise and eat, because the journey is too great for you" (1 Kings 19:7, *NKJV*). And what happened? "So he [Elijah] arose, and ate and drank; and he went in the strength of that food forty days and forty nights as far as Horeb, the mountain of God" (1 Kings 19:8, *NKJV*).

Like Elijah and young Lynn from the puppet ministry, you may find that a simple afternoon snack before sundown helps you fulfill God's call to fast.

Fast with a Purpose

Before you fast, search your heart to determine the reason you are fasting. The best way to search your heart is to write down the purpose of your fast. There's an old adage that goes, "Thoughts disentangle themselves over lips and fingertips." Sometimes our written purpose perfectly reflects our heart. But other times, our thinking is not very clear. By changing the words or rewriting the sentence, you can sharpen and bring focus to your purpose. You may have three or four reasons why you are fasting. Write down each and determine which is the most important, putting them in order of priority. If you don't write them down, your objectives may remain blurred or vague. But when you put your purpose in writing, you know exactly what's at stake.

A fast is not easy. It's spiritual warfare. When you fast and pray, you take on the forces of hell. Even Satan's demons will try to stop you. Assume the attitude that you're going to war and have a clear objective for your battle.

When young David went to fight Goliath, he knew why he was fighting: "Is there not a cause?" (1 Sam. 17:29, *NKJV*). The other soldiers tried to stop David from fighting Goliath. Not only would *they* not fight the giant, but also they gave David all kinds of reasons why *he* should not fight the huge Philistine. Like those Israelite soldiers, friends may try to talk you out of your fast. But if you know why you are fasting, you can say with David, "Is there not a cause?"

What you're about to do is more than giving up food. It's more than spending time on your knees. God has called you to a higher purpose. You're fasting for a cause. When the battle becomes intense, knowing your cause will help you stay the course with purpose and sincerity.

Following is a fasting checklist. Just as a pilot goes through a flight checklist before takeoff to ensure her plane arrives safely at its destination, so too your checklist will help you complete your fast successfully. The pilot already knows to do the tasks on the list, but checking off the items one by one gives her confidence to fly. Wouldn't you like to pray with confidence?

Plan Your Fast

Don't enter into your fast casually. When you go on a driving vacation, you plan a route, where you will lodge and perhaps even where you will stop for meals. You might even make a budget. Take the same approach with fasting. Write out your plans, including your destination, how you will get there, where you will pray and what you will do during mealtimes.

There was a missionary in South America who was not hungry for breakfast. Then he got busy and didn't eat all day. That night he decided to see how long he could fast, wondering if he could go 40 days but without a particular goal in mind or a plan for getting there. Each day his fast progressed without a destination. When he got to day 14, he stopped. In his journal he wrote, "I know I cannot go 40 days." The problem is that he didn't make a plan to fast for 40 days—he was just fasting to see how long he could make it. What did he find out? He could only make it 14 days. Like that missionary, if you begin fasting just to see how long you can hold out or to find out what it feels like, you will likely fail.

Some people say, "I'll fast until I get hungry." At the first sign of discomfort, they give up. I'm not sure that deserves to be called fasting! I'd call it waiting too long to eat. Anyone who fasts gets hungry.

Fasting Checklist

Purpose: ______________________________

____

____

Fast (what I will withhold): ______________________________

____

____

Begin: Date __________ Time ______________________________
End: Date __________ Time ______________________________

My Bible promise: ______________________________

____

____

Resources (what I need for this fast): ______________________________

____

____

Vow: I believe God's involvement is the only answer to my need and that prayer without fasting is not enough to get an answer. Therefore, I am fasting by faith because I need God to work in this matter. **God being my strength and grace being my basis, I commit myself to the above fast.**

____

Signature

That is the point. Physical hunger is a tangible, very real reminder of our hunger for God and for His intervention in our lives. Make a commitment that you will make it through a one-day fast no matter what. Use the checklist to help you think through your journey and destination before you leave the comforts of home. While filling out a checklist does not guarantee you will be successful, you are much more likely to reach your destination if you think through your journey. Why? Because you are prepared for the twists, turns and obstacles that lie between you and a successful fast. When discomfort and difficulty arise, you are not surprised. You are prepared.

A Fast Is a Vow

On your checklist, there is a vow for you to sign. This is not a legalistic document; it is covenant between you and God. You are making a commitment to seek the Lord and entreat His blessing on your life.

"I hope I can make it through" is not a vow. Neither is "I think I can make this work." No, a vow is a commitment in heart, mind and soul to the completion of the project. You are asking for God's presence, and you are entering into partnership with God to meet your need. According to Paul, "We are labourers together with God" (1 Cor. 3:9, *KJV*). Isn't it wonderful to be a co-laborer with God?

Your vow is not a bargain with God. There are some people who wrongly think they can "make a deal." It goes something like this: "God, if I don't eat for three days, will You heal my friend's cancer?" Fasting is nothing like a deal. It's not a transaction. That's legalism!

You are fasting based on the grace of God. In His grace, God forgives our sins because we cry out to Him in the name of Jesus Christ, not because we do good works to earn salvation. In the same way, we cry out in prayer and fasting for God's grace to answer our prayers. A vow to fast is a promise to trust God's grace to sustain your physical needs through your fast *and* to answer your prayer. When you sign a vow, you are saying that God is going to do it all, and that you will accept whatever answer He sends. You are promising to trust that God, in His grace, will give you what is best.

If you've made a plan and filled out your checklist, you're almost ready to begin. But first you must decide what kind of fast to undertake. So read on . . .

4

Six Ways to Fast

Fasting begins in the heart with a passion to know God. And because hunger for God is its wellspring, fasting is rarely a one-time event. Rather, for many believers, it becomes a regular habit in their vibrant pursuit of God. But not everybody fasts in the same way; in fact, many believers fast in different ways at different times. The reason is simple.

The Bible doesn't lay out rules on how to fast. It offers no formulas for fasting. Instead, Scripture *describes* what various believers do when they have a passion to know God. As a result, we see people fasting in many different ways, doing many different things—and the things they do are not always consistent. If we take the full testimony of Scripture, we must conclude there is no single correct way to fast. We find instead that God is not as concerned with the way we fast as He is with our attitude when we fast.

This chapter offers six different ways to fast. Whichever method you choose, approach your fast in humble trust that God will meet your needs.

1. The "Normal" or Juice Fast

In the "normal" fast, individuals stop eating solid food. A biblical example of the normal fast is Yom Kippur: "On the tenth day of the seventh month of each year, you must go without eating to show sorrow for your sins" (Lev. 16:29, *CEV*). The Bible indicates that some people drank liquids during the fast, but it doesn't tell us what they drank. It may have been water, milk, the juice of various fruits or a liquid form of desert cacti. Hence, people who undertake a normal fast today have freedom to decide what liquids they will drink while they fast from solid food.

The normal fast usually lasts for one day, three days or a week. Longer fasts are possible but should be undertaken only after plenty of practice with shorter fasts. Remember, you must train to run a marathon! After many years of shorter fasts, I once fasted for 40 days by drinking a glass of orange juice in the morning and a glass of V8 juice in the evening. During the day, I drank water and coffee.

I have been criticized for drinking coffee during a fast because it is a stimulant. To me, coffee is just the liquid I drink in the morning! When I fast, I drink a hot cup around six am, then I keep coffee on my desk to sip throughout the morning hours. About once an hour, I take a sip of coffee—even after it's cold. At that point, I'm not drinking coffee because I like it or because it is a stimulant. I'm drinking it to keep my mouth and throat moist! To those who criticize drinking coffee during a fast, I offer the following reminder: God is more concerned about the prayers that come out of our hearts than He is about the liquid that goes into our bodies.

Whether you choose fruit and vegetable juices, milk, coffee or tea, or water only, decide in advance what liquids you will allow during your fast. Use your fasting checklist to ensure you have supplied yourself with the resources you will need to stay both hydrated and committed.

2. The Absolute Fast

When they undertake an absolute fast, people do not eat solid food or drink liquids of any kind. No one should ever follow an absolute fast for more than two or three days. Medical authorities say that after six or seven days with no liquid, your physical organism shuts down. That is, you die. But long before that seven days is up, you'll do permanent damage to your brain. Water is essential to life and you cannot survive without it.

Three days is the limit for an absolute fast. If you decide to undertake this kind of fast, drink plenty of water in the days leading up to your launch. This will help to ensure you stay hydrated and healthy for the one, two or three days you are fasting. You should also be sensible about your activities during your fast. Don't workout or play sports, or do any other activity that causes you to sweat heavily or get overheated. When your body sweats, it loses water that must be replenished—something you have vowed not to do! Fasting is demanding enough for your body. Don't overtax it with activities that can wait until your fast is complete.

3. The Daniel Fast

The Daniel fast is sometimes called a partial fast. In this fast, certain foods are omitted or certain foods are eaten on a modified schedule. Those who fast in this way may also abstain from certain activities.

As a young Hebrew man, Daniel was taken as an exile from conquered Judah to Babylon, where he was "retrained" to serve in the court of Nebuchadnezzar. Part of his retraining was a special diet designed to acculturate Jewish young men into the Babylonian culture. The goal was for the Jewish exiles to live by Babylonian laws, values and customs, and to eat Babylonian food. "The king appointed for them [Daniel and his three friends] a daily provision of the king's delicacies and of the wine which he drank" (Dan. 1:5, *NKJV*).

Daniel and his friends asked to be excused from eating the meat and drinking the wine (see Dan. 1:11-14). The Bible says, "Daniel purposed in his heart that he would not defile himself with the portion of the king's delicacies, nor with the wine" (Dan. 1:8, *NKJV*). Notice the word "purposed." The secret to Daniel's successful fast was his vow not to eat what the king provided.

Why did Daniel ask to be excused? Scripture does not say. Perhaps the food had been offered to idols and eating it would legitimize the Babylonian gods. Perhaps the wine was highly intoxicating and drinking it would lead to drunkenness. Perhaps the food included non-kosher meats, which violated Jewish dietary laws. Perhaps he merely had a desire for good health, but it seems more likely that he wanted to keep his body separate to God. (Isn't that one of the reasons you fast?) Whatever the case, Daniel knew that Babylonian food and drink was off limits. He did not want to compromise his way of life, dedicated to honoring Yahweh, for a new culture.

So what did Daniel do? The young man said to his trainers, "Prove thy servants, I beseech thee, ten days; and let them give us pulse to eat, and water to drink" (Dan. 1:12, *KJV*). Most of the newer translations use the word "vegetables" instead of "pulse." The original Hebrew word probably refers to leafy vegetables such as lettuce, turnip greens, cabbage, spinach, and so on. Daniel went on a salad diet! And what happened? "At the end of ten days their features appeared better and fatter in flesh than all the young men who ate the portion of the king's delicacies" (Dan. 1:15, *NKJV*).

While Daniel's first fast in Babylon was for 10 days, he later fasted for 21 days (see Dan. 10). Because of the prophet's example, what we call the Daniel fast is *a time fast for a specific purpose.* (The purpose of Daniel's 10-day fast was to prove God's sufficiency to his trainers; his second was to receive a vision from God; see Dan.

10:1-3.) You decide how long you will fast, along with the purpose for which you are fasting. I have been on a one-day Daniel fast, a three-day Daniel fast and a 40-day Daniel fast. Each time, I fasted for a specific purpose.

In the record of Daniel's 21-day fast, he said, "I ate no pleasant food, no meat or wine came into my mouth" (Dan. 10:3, *NKJV*). The word translated "pleasant food" in this verse probably means things we consider enjoyable, such as steak broiled over an open fire, escargot, veal cutlets with provolone, or a baked Alaska. The *NIV* translates this word as "choicest food"; the *CEV* calls it "fancy food"; the *CSV* and the *TLB* use "rich food." The Daniel fast is giving up things you enjoy, while you eat or do only what is necessary. Here are some different ways the Daniel fast is celebrated:

- **Eat one meal a day and spend the other mealtimes in prayer.** Perhaps they are thinking of Jesus' exhortation, "Could you not watch with Me one hour?" (Matt. 26:40, *NKJV*). It takes about one hour to eat a meal served in a restaurant or eaten at home, so one hour of prayer and meditation is recommended for each skipped meal.
- **Eat only vegetables.** Daniel gave up all other food groups except vegetables. While this is a good fast, it doesn't set aside time to pray. It assumes that you will eat vegetables at mealtime and pray at other times during the day.
- **Give up television for a limited time.** Unsaved people may hear you have given up television and laugh at you. But this is a commitment of time: You're going to take back the hours you spend in front of the TV and instead spend time with God. It's also a spiritual fast, practicing putting Christ first. "Seek first the kingdom of God and His righteousness, and all these things shall be added to you" (Matt. 6:33, *NKJV*).

- **Give up sports for a limited time.** Participation in sports is good for us, not only because it helps keep us fit but also because it can help us grow in character when we practice teamwork and good sportsmanship. However, giving up participation in sports for a period of time can have great results spiritually if we spend that time in intercession and prayer. You choose to put spiritual exercise before physical exercise. Paul said, "Bodily exercise profits a little, but godliness is profitable for all things" (1 Tim. 4:8, *NKJV*).
- **Give up pleasure reading.** There are things we must read for our job, to prepare a Sunday school lesson or for other obligations. However, there are things we read in our spare time for relaxation and enjoyment. This can be reading a novel, the newspaper, a magazine, or material from the Internet. For a limited time, set aside reading and spend time in prayer.
- **Restrict smartphone use and text messaging.** While using hi-tech communications may be necessary at times, they are also serious time-wasters. When you give them up during a fast, spend the time in prayer. Time spent in the presence of God is better than time chatting with friends or playing with apps and games.
- **Give up music.** You may want to restrict pleasure music, listening only to Christian music while fasting. You can use Christian music for praise, worship and meditation. But eliminate secular music that takes your mind off Christ.

4. The John Wesley Fast

This is a fast that was practiced by John Wesley, the founder of Methodism, leading up to the monthly ministerial conference where pastors gathered for revival. For 10 days, John Wesley and other leaders ate bread (whole grains) and drank water as they prayed and prepared sermons to preach to the preachers. This type of fast is especially effective for preparing for ministry.

The ministers in the early Methodist church were not well trained; almost none had college or seminary education. They were called "plow-boy" preachers or "shop-keep" preachers. Most Methodist preachers had not prepared academically for ministry, but when they felt called of God they obeyed, leaving their trades to preach the gospel. The early Methodist church was more concerned about spiritual power than it was about ecclesiastical formats.

Most of these ministers were circuit-riding preachers who went out on horseback for 24 to 26 days at a time. Most looked after 20 to 40 local congregations. They usually preached the same sermon over and over to every church on their circuit, then gathered with the other circuit preachers to receive a fresh word from the Lord. John Wesley gathered leaders such as Francis Asbury, George Whitfield, Joe Parker and Charles Wesley to teach and instruct them. The leaders would preach one sermon after another and the circuit preachers would take copious notes, writing down everything they heard. When the conference was over, the circuit riders were refreshed and had new material to continue their preaching ministry to dozens of churches.

Wesley and the other Methodist leaders made a habit of fasting for 10 days before these monthly conferences. They knew that the word they brought to the circuit riders would be passed on to hundreds, if not thousands, of others—so it was of paramount importance to make sure every sermon was birthed in fasting and prayer. This grounding in spiritual discipline led to explosive growth in the early Methodist church. When the Revolutionary War began in 1775, there were 243 Methodist churches in the United States. By the war of 1812, there were more than 5,000. Fasting leaders produce growing churches.

5. The Rotational or Mayo Clinic Fast

This is primarily a medical fast to determine causes of sickness or other physical ailment. The patient begins with an absolute fast, not eating anything for 24 hours. This is to cleanse the systems of the body. Each following day (or sometimes longer) he eats from only one of the food groups. In this way, doctors attempt to isolate the causes of physical problems associated with particular foods.

There is little spiritual reason to choose the rotational fast over one of the other types, but if you are prescribed this type of fast by your doctor you can undertake it as a spiritual exercise as well as a medical necessity. It would certainly be a good time to pray for God's healing touch! During the first 24 hours, spend mealtimes in prayer as you would on a normal, absolute or Daniel fast. On subsequent days, set aside time to pray during or between meals. You may also consider asking for anointing and prayer from your church's pastor or elders before your fast begins.

6. The Supernatural Fast

There are a few descriptions in Scripture of fasts that extended far past the point at which someone would die had not God sustained them supernaturally. Jesus wandered in the desert for 40 days, during which time He ate no food (see Matt. 4:1-11). He may have drunk spring water or juice from desert cacti; Scripture does not say. Elijah traveled for 40 days to Mount Horeb without eating, after a meal provided by an angel of the Lord (see 1 Kings 19:1-8). Moses fasted for 40 days, neither eating nor drinking any liquid (see Exod. 34:28). While this is commendable, it is also supernatural. No one can survive 40 days without water. God did the miraculous in Moses' case.

Should you follow Moses' 40-day fast from both food and water, believing God will do the same for you? No. God is too good to tell us to do anything that would hurt our bodies. He wants us to care for our bodies, to honor Him through our bodies (see 1 Cor. 6:13-20). As I wrote in the introduction to this chapter, many stories in the Bible are *descriptive*. They describe what people did, including not drinking water for 40 days. But not all Bible stories are *prescriptive*, that is, a command for us to follow their example. As we read Scripture together, we must use discernment under the Holy Spirit's guidance to identify descriptive and prescriptive stories and to avoid confusing the two.

In a very real sense, every fast is supernatural. We are trusting God to sustain us and to answer our prayers—both supernatural activities! In order to honor God by taking responsible care of the bodies He has given us, we should avoid absolute fasts longer than three days, even as we recognize that our God is able to do the miraculous. As Jesus said to His tempter, Satan: "It is also written: 'Do not put the Lord your God to the test'" (Matt. 4:7). Let's fast in such a way that we demonstrate our faith in God without testing Him.

Which Fast Is Right for You?

You may try various types of fasts at different times for different purposes. And that's great! The point of this chapter is that there's no single "right" way to fast.

As you consider various ways of fasting, pray for the Spirit's guidance in choosing the right type for you and your circumstances. Talk to your doctor if you have medical concerns about withholding food, and talk with your pastor or other spiritual mentor if you are uncertain which fasting method is best for you.

Once you have decided what type of fast to undertake, you are ready to complete your checklist and launch your fast. But what does it mean to fast with the Lord's Prayer? Find out in the next section . . .

Part II

The Seven Petitions of the Lord's Prayer

The "Thy" Petitions

Thy Name Be Hallowed: A Worship Experience
Thy Kingdom Come: A Majestic Experience
Thy Will Be Done: A Submissive Experience

Jesus taught His disciples to pray by teaching them a prayer, which we call the Lord's Prayer. The focus of the Lord's Prayer is God, not the person who is praying. Begin with worship: "Thy Name be hallowed." Then pray to expand God's reign on earth: "Thy kingdom come." Next, surrender your life to God: "Thy will be done."

The Middle Petition

Give Us Our Daily Bread: A Dependent Experience

Only one out of seven petitions is a plea for God to meet fundamental needs: "Give us our daily bread."

The "Us" Petitions

Forgive Us Our Debts: A Cleansing Experience
Lead Us Not into Temptation: A Victorious Experience
Deliver Us from the Evil One: A Triumphant Experience

The final three petitions are for fellowship with God. Pray that intimacy with God would be restored: "Forgive us our debts." Then pray for victory in spiritual warfare: "Lead us not into temptation." Next, pray for divine protection: "Deliver us from the Evil One."

Conclude by recognizing God's good reign and unparalleled power, and by acknowledging that the glory is His for all answered prayer: "Thine is the kingdom, the power and the glory forever."

5

Invocation: Our Father Who Art in Heaven

When Jesus taught us to pray, He didn't tell us to begin, "Our Lord, who art in heaven." That would have recognized God's lordship and sovereignty, but Jesus promised something better.

He didn't tell us to begin, "Our God, who art in heaven." That would have recognized that God is the Creator of the universe and we are His creatures, but Jesus promised something better.

He didn't tell us to begin, "Our Master in heaven." That would have recognized God's control over our lives, but Jesus promised something better.

He didn't tell us to begin, "Our King, who art in heaven." That would have recognized God's rule over us and the urgency of expanding His kingdom, but Jesus promised something better.

He didn't tell us to pray, "Our Shepherd, who art in heaven." That would have recognized God's care for and protection over us, but Jesus promised something better.

Rather than telling His followers to use any of those Old Testament images of God, Jesus tells us to address Him with a new name. It was the name Jesus Himself had used throughout past ages in heaven. It was His special name for the First Person of the Trinity—and now Jesus invites us to talk to God with the same intimacy, affection and familiarity with which He prayed! "Our Father, who art in heaven."

Praying with Jesus

Let's jump from the beginning of the Lord's Prayer to the end. Notice that it does not end "in Jesus' name." That's the way most of us end our prayers today. Some extreme dispensationalists say we shouldn't pray the Lord's Prayer because it doesn't end "in Jesus' name." Why? Because Jesus said, "And whatsoever ye shall ask in my name, that will I do" (John 14:13, *KJV*).

When Jesus told us to pray in His name (see also John 15:7,16; 16:24), did He mean that we must always use His exact words to conclude our prayers? I know a man who always begins his prayer, "I pray in Jesus' name and call upon Jesus to answer my prayer . . ." He is certainly praying in Jesus' name, but does it make a difference that it comes at the beginning instead of the end?

For that matter, the Lord's Prayer doesn't begin *or* end in Jesus' name! Does that mean we shouldn't pray it at all?

No! Look at the first word in the Lord's Prayer. *Our.* The word "our" is, of course, plural, and includes the person who is praying and at least one other person. Many high church Christians such as Lutherans, Presbyterians and Anglicans pray the Lord's Prayer every Sunday in their services. When they pray, "Our Father," they are including all the worshipers in the service who are praying with them, and perhaps other believers around the world. While it is wonderful to recognize the communal aspect of prayer, that's not the primary meaning of "our" in the prayer Jesus taught us.

When you pray, "Our Father," you are declaring that you and Jesus are coming together to the heavenly Father. "Our" means Jesus and you. Besides fulfilling the requirement to pray in Jesus' name, understanding the "our" in this way has tremendous biblical resonance.

"Our" declares that Jesus Christ is in your heart and the two of you are praying together (see Gal. 2:20). "Our" claims the benefits of Jesus' death on the cross for you; you were positionally in Jesus Christ when He died, and now you are coming to the Father through the blood of Jesus Christ (see Rom. 6:5-6; 1 John 1:7). "Our" acknowledges that you are praying through Jesus Christ, who intercedes for us at the right hand of the Father (see Heb. 7:24-25). "Our" claims Jesus as your advocate, the righteous lawyer who pleads your case before the holy Judge (see 1 John 2:1-2). You pray the words, but Jesus presents your petitions to the Father.

But what does fasting have to do with this? Fasting demonstrates there's nothing standing between you and the Lord Jesus Christ. Your passion is not food, money, your career, your stuff, your family or any other earthly thing. You fast to put Jesus first in your life. And as you fast in the presence of God, you come to a place of surrender: "Thy will be done." When you have yielded to Christ, He is able to change your perspective, and even change your requests to align more closely with God's will. Prayer and fasting are not only to convince God to change others or change the world; sometimes fasting and prayer will change *you*. You begin because you need an urgent answer to prayer and end up transformed in the presence of God. That is the power of the Lord's Prayer.

What's in a Name?

My mother was a McFadden from South Carolina. When I was a small boy, she would take me to the McFadden Cemetery on the banks of the Black River in Clarendon County. It was surrounded by cotton and tobacco fields, and you could see two or three farmhouses in the distance. Mother always reminded us that the McFadden family had cleared the land, built houses and barns, and made great lives for themselves out of practically nothing. One Memorial Day when I was about 12 years old, we spent all day cleaning up the cemetery for our relatives. At the end of the day, Mother stood my sister and me before a huge 10-foot granite stone that listed 200 years of McFadden ancestors. The list was topped by those who had settled that part of the country, beginning with James McFadden from the days of the Revolutionary War. Under his name were many succeeding generations, right down to my grandfather, Robert E. Lee McFadden, Jr.

As we gazed at that engraved marker, Mother said, "Remember, you've got McFadden blood flowing in your veins. Make me proud of you." Mother didn't ask; she commanded. "You're better than most because you've got McFadden blood. Now go and make a name for yourself."

Call her an elitist if you must, but all my life I felt the burden of that encounter. I've always felt that I must do my best and excel in everything I do. Why? Because of the McFadden name. I've got McFadden blood flowing in my veins.

As a Christian, you have a greater burden.

You have the name of your heavenly Father upon your life. You belong to the God of heaven. He is your Father. That makes you special. Your heavenly Father loves you, and He has a special purpose for you, a purpose only you can fulfill. That's a lot to live up to! But the very presence of God will enable you to become the son or daughter the Father made you to be.

Just as an earthly father finds teachable moments to guide his children when they go wrong, so too your heavenly Father will allow problems and difficulties to come into your life to teach and strengthen you. Just as an earthly father grabs his child by the hand to keep him from darting into traffic, so too your heavenly Father keeps you from danger. Just as a good earthly father knows that too much stuff may spoil a child and make her self-centered, so too your heavenly Father sometimes says no to the stuff you ask for in prayer.

Get to know God as your Father. Call on Him by His name. Learn what it means to be His child.

A Radical New Name

The Old Testament Jews didn't call God by the name "Father." They used the image of a father as a metaphor to understand His character, along with other images such as a warrior, a shepherd, a husband and even a mother. But they did not call God "Father." Instead, the Scriptures refer to God by three primary names or titles.

The first is *Elohim*, a Hebrew word that means "Mighty Creator." "In the beginning [Elohim] created the heavens and the earth" (Gen. 1:1, *NKJV*). We are made in the image of God: "So [Elohim] created man in His own image, in the image of [Elohim] created He him, male and female created He them" (Gen. 1:27, *NKJV*). Like Him, we each have an intellect, emotions, a will and a personality. And like Him, we have the ability and the drive to create.

The second name for God is *Adonai*, which means "Master" and is translated "Lord" (only the first letter is capitalized in our Bibles). Adonai owns and rules us; we are His slaves. He is the One we should obey (see Gen. 15). This is the name by which observant Jews call God in prayer and when they read the Torah (the first five books of the Bible), to avoid saying Yahweh.

The third name for God is *Yahweh*. The Jews did not (and do not) say this name aloud, and do not spell it out completely. When ancient Jewish scholars were copying the Old Testament, they selected a new pen with which to write the abbreviation of Yahweh so as not to dishonor God by writing His name with a used pen. Then they broke the new pen, never to use it again. That's because Yahweh is holy (see Lev. 11:45). Each instance in our English translations where you see the word "Lord" in small capital letters is a place where Jewish copyists abbreviated Yahweh in the ancient manuscripts.

Yahweh is the covenant-keeping One, the One who relates to His people. In Genesis 2, it is Yahweh who breathes life into the first human being and then makes a mate suitable for him—both intimate, relational acts (see Gen. 2:7-25). It is Yahweh who calls Abram out of Ur to become the father of God's chosen people (see Gen. 12). It is Yahweh who rescues the children of Israel from slavery in Egypt and gives them the Law to make them a new nation (see Exod. 20).

There are three primary names for God in the Old Testament, but there is only one God: "The Lord our God is one Lord" (Deut. 6:4, *KJV*). And it is this One God whom Jesus invites His followers to call Father! This was a radical change from centuries of Jewish practice.

When you pray to our Father in heaven, as Jesus taught, you are claiming your relationship with and access to God. You are claiming family intimacy. What is intimacy? When you are intimate with a spouse, parent or friend, what do you feel? You feel *one with them*. You feel *together*, that you are thinking together, working together, and that you have the same purpose. You experience your love relationship on an emotional and spiritual level, not just cognitively. Likewise, when you pray, "Our Father who art in heaven," you are opening yourself to experience a relationship of love with the Mighty Creator, the Lord of the Universe, the Lord of the Covenant. Calling God Father is the greatest privilege in the world. What a gift!

6

First Petition: Hallowed Be Thy Name

Sometimes when you pray, you feel as though your prayers are bouncing off the ceiling. They can't get through, as if the ceiling is made of lead. You enter your prayer closet and feel as if you're talking only to yourself. You don't feel close to God. You don't sense His presence with you.

Other times, you step onto praying ground and feel instantly connected to the Father. You talk to Him and know that He is listening. He even talks back through the still, small voice of His Spirit.

Why these different experiences?

Remember, Jesus said, "The Father is seeking . . . worship" (John 4:23, *NKJV*). When you begin to pray, God's localized presence in heaven is listening to all the prayers of all of His people from all around the world. But then you begin to worship with all your heart. You're weeping. You're begging. You're banging on the windows of heaven. And God says to the angels, "Let's go down and get close to this person who is worshiping Me." God comes close to receive your worship.

The 1988 film *Field of Dreams* tells the story of a farmer from Iowa who keeps hearing voices. They whisper, "If you build it, they will come." He can't get the voices out of his mind, and finally he builds a baseball field smack in the middle of his corn field. When it is finished, great baseball heroes from the past emerge from the rows of corn to play on the field.

If you worship the Father, He will come. An empty ball field is irresistible to a lover of the game, but it's nothing compared to the sacrifice of your worship to the heavenly Father. God's presence will visit your room or closet when you worship.

Every time you pray, "Hallowed be Thy name," you are worshiping the Father. We don't use "hallowed" much anymore, so let's be sure we know what it means. When someone describes the "hallowed halls of Congress," for example, they are saying the U.S. Capitol Building is a place that deserves respect. Some would even say we must be reverent in those halls. When you pray, "Hallowed by Thy name," you are offering the Father your respect and reverence. You are recognizing His worth. You are joining the angels who surround the throne crying, "Holy, holy, holy" (Isa. 6:3, *NKJV*).

Acknowledge God's Worth

What is worship? Worship is giving to God the worth-ship due to Him. God is Elohim, the Mighty Creator, and we exalt Him because of the great power and glory we see in the natural world—a world that also exalts Him: "The heavens declare the glory of God" (Ps. 19:1, *NKJV*). That's worship.

God is Adonai, the Lord of all, and we lift Him up as the Master worth obeying, not only because He is all-powerful but also because He is good. "You have dealt well with your servant, O Lord, according to Your word. . . . You are good, and do good; teach me Your statutes" (Ps. 119:65,68, *NKJV*). That's worship.

God is Yahweh, the Covenant-keeper, and we bow in the presence of the Lord because He came to establish an eternal relationship with us. Moses bowed before the bush that burned with fire but was not consumed. He took off his shoes and fell on his face, prostrate on the ground (see Exod. 3:1-6). We bow before the same Lord, who today deserves our reverence and worship for all He has done to redeem His people. That's worship.

When did worship begin? In the first moments of creation: "In the beginning God created the heavens and the earth" (Gen 1:1, *NKJV*). According to Psalm 19, the heavens declare God's glory—so the very moment God brought them into being, worship began. The "heavens" includes all the planets and the trillions upon trillions of stars, each a burning sun, as well as our atmosphere and the heaven of heavens, which is the dwelling place of God. Heaven is not an eternal place; according to Genesis 1, God created it. That also means God's throne is not eternal, nor are the angels. They were also created in the beginning, and their main duty is to worship and praise God. They were created to cry, "Holy, holy, holy."

Worship is the most fundamental response of humans and angels to God. It's the reason God created us. The Westminster Shorter Catechism asks, "What is the chief end of man?" The answer is simple: "To glorify God, and to enjoy him forever." We know the "heavens declare the glory of God," but God is also glorified by the people He created who praise His name. The heavens have no choice but to worship God; they are objects without a will. But we have a choice. God has given each and every human a free will. You can choose to obey God, or not. You can choose righteousness or sin. You can choose to do God's will, or you can choose to do your own.

When you freely choose to worship the Father, exalting His hallowed name, He comes to receive your worship. He is there whether you "feel" Him or not; but in my experience, worshiping, fasting and praying with the Lord's Prayer often leads to a felt experience of God's presence. I call this His "atmospheric presence." Praying the Lord's Prayer, I often feel His presence, though I am the only physical presence in the room. I can hear His voice in my heart, though there is no audible sound.

As you learn to pray and fast the Lord's Prayer, my prayer is that you too will experience God's atmospheric presence in a life-changing way.

Hallow God's Name in Your Life

When you pray, "Hallowed be Thy name," you are lifting up God's name in praise, but you are also asking to show His name holy in your life. What does this look like in practice?

After the children of Israel built a golden calf and began to worship it instead of Yahweh, who had brought them out of Egypt, God told Moses He would no longer lead the people as a pillar of fire and cloud (see Exod. 33:1-3). His angel would lead them to the Promised Land, because of His covenant with Abraham, but the presence of God would not go before them. This was very bad news, especially for Moses, who relied on God's strength and power to help him lead the troublesome children of Israel. So Moses stood on the mountain and prayed for God's glory to come down (see Exod. 33:18). He knew that if God abandoned him, there was no hope.

Is that where you are today? Are you standing on the mountaintop, asking for God's glory to come down?

God answered Moses' prayer. He hid Moses in the cleft of a rock because "You cannot see My face; no man shall see Me, and live" (Exod. 33:20, *NKJV*). When His presence passed by, Moses caught a glimpse of His back. And the Lord said, "The Lord, the Lord God, merciful and gracious, longsuffering, and abounding in goodness and truth, keeping mercy for thousands, forgiving iniquity and transgression and sin" (Exod. 34:6-7, *NKJV*).

God revealed His glory to Moses. But more than that, He revealed His character. He is holy, set apart, completely "Other," because His mercy, grace, patience, goodness, truth and forgiveness are far beyond what we humans can even imagine.

To show the holiness of His name in your life means nurturing the same character in yourself. When you pray, "Hallowed be Thy name," you are asking God to refine and shape you into a person whose character reflects His. You are asking Him to make you merciful, gracious, patient, good, truthful and forgiving.

God shapes our character through many different means, not least through prayer, fasting and worship. As we spend more time in His presence, we begin to hear His Spirit speaking to our spirit. In order for this to happen, we have to listen! How can He speak to us if we never let Him get a word in edgewise? Let's heed His command: "Be still, and know that I am God" (Ps. 46:10). When we are quiet in His presence, God can speak.

Isn't that what Elijah had to learn? After his confrontation with the priests of Baal, Elijah complained to God about the difficulties he had recently survived. The prophet had worked diligently to serve God, demonstrating His supreme power to pagan priests and wayward Israelites (see 1 Kings 18:16-45). All he got for his trouble were death threats and manhunts! "I have been very zealous for the Lord God of hosts; for the children of Israel have forsaken Your covenant, torn down Your altars, and killed Your prophets with the sword. I alone am left; and they seek to take my life" (1 Kings 19:10, *NKJV*). On and on he went, ranting and raving about his situation.

But once Elijah ran out of breath, what happened?

> Behold, the Lord passed by, and a great and strong wind tore into the mountains and broke the rocks in pieces before the

> Lord, but the Lord was not in the wind; and after the wind an earthquake, but the Lord was not in the earthquake; and after the earthquake a fire, but the Lord was not in the fire; and after the fire a still small voice (1 Kings 19:11-12, *NKJV*).

Elijah was still upset about his circumstances, but now he remembered to listen for God's voice. Once he got quiet enough to listen, God told the prophet exactly what he needed to do next (see 1 Kings 19:14-18).

Sometimes we can't hear God speaking to us because we are too busy complaining to Him. We must get quiet in His presence. Then He will speak softly. We must listen carefully to hear what He is saying. As we become better listeners, He will show us how to manifest His holiness in our lives.

Fast to Hallow God's Name

One morning I woke up early to pray. I had been fasting about a personnel problem at Liberty University, praying about whether to keep a professor or let him go.

Right before the sun came up, I met with God. Outside my window I could see dew on the grass and I prayed the words of an old gospel song:

> I come to the garden alone
> While the dew is still on the roses,
> And the voice I hear falling on my ear
> The Son of God discloses.
> And He walks with me, and He talks with me,
> And He tells me I am His own;
> And the joy we share as we tarry there
> None other has ever known.[1]

I forgot about my personnel problem and began worshiping God. As I did, I felt God's presence in the room. He was beside me to receive my worship.

I began worshiping God by exalting His many names. I worshiped Jesus Christ by calling out as many names for Him as I could remember, giving Jesus glory for what each of His names means. I continued to worship by exalting many of the names for the Father. I thanked Him for all of His Old Testament titles and what they mean for me. And because I am a Trinitarian, I couldn't leave out the Holy Spirit! So I began worshiping the Spirit by giving glory to as many of His names that I could remember.[2]

The Lord filled that room to receive my worship. And I became so focused on God that I forgot my prayer request about the faculty member. The Lord was so close! I was brushing His face with worship, and in return He was brushing my heart with His presence. As that rich time of communion drew to a close, I remembered the request that had brought me to fast and pray in the first place. So I offered a quick prayer that God would show me what to do about the faculty member, and then went to work for the day.

A short time later, a local pastor and a member of his staff came to see me to testify about the godly spiritual impact the faculty member was making in their church. Because of that testimony, the faculty member kept his position and has gone on to serve God in a wonderful way.

When God's presence comes into a room, you don't have to spend a lot of time begging for an answer to prayer. You may decide to fast because of an urgent request for God's intervention, but if you focus on Him instead of your need, your life will change. That morning, I touched God and He touched me—and I could never be the same. Now I can never be content with just reading my Bible and praying through my requests. Each morning, I must meet God; and God wants to meet me.

Remember what happened when Isaiah encountered the Lord: "I saw the Lord. He was sitting on a lofty throne, and the train of his robe filled the Temple" (Isa. 6:1, *NLT*). Because the Temple is mentioned, I imagine Isaiah praying in that holy place. He may have seen the smoke of incense ascending from the altar into heaven, a picture of prayers ascending to God. The smoke rose and wrapped itself around the robe of the heavenly King, a glorious train that filled the Temple and overwhelmed Isaiah. After that encounter, the prophet was never the same (see Isa. 6:5-8).

Just one encounter with God and you will never go back to playing games with fasting and prayer. Each time you meet with Him, your spirit will rise to new levels of worship and praise.

Once your fast is over, you will again feed on earthly food; you need food to grow. But once you let the Bread of Life satisfy you, you will hunger to taste His presence again and again. Fasting will ruin your appetite for superficial prayer.

When you pray, "Hallowed be Thy name," you are stepping into God's throne room. You enter into God's presence, where His reign is complete. You come humbly to the sovereign Lord of the universe, and it's not about you and your demands. You come to worship God, to glorify and manifest His holy name in prayer, in fasting and in your life.

As you worship and exalt His names—Mighty Creator, King, Lord of all—the Father comes near and draws you to His heart. There on His lap, you tell Him how much you love and adore Him. And just as a loving earthly father is concerned about the needs and hurts of his child, so too your Father in heaven concerns Himself with your needs and hurts. Those times of communion will change you.

Notes

1. Charles Austin Miles, "In the Garden," 1912. http://www.hymnlyrics.org/mostpopular hymns/inthegarden.php (accessed February 2013).
2. See Elmer Towns, *The Names of Jesus* (Colorado Springs, CO: Accent Books, 1997). This book examines more than 725 names for Jesus. See also Elmer Towns, *My Father's Names* (Ventura, CA: Regal Books, 1991). This book examines more than 100 names for the Father. See also Elmer Towns, *The Names of the Holy Spirit* (Ventura, CA: Regal Books, 1996). There are 126 names for the Holy Spirit, each name revealing a facet of what the Holy Spirit does for believers. No one had written a book on the names of the Holy Spirit prior to this publication. It won the Gold Medallion Award in 1997.

7

Second Petition: Thy Kingdom Come

When you pray, "Thy kingdom come," you are asking that the gospel would spread to those who do not yet follow Christ. "Thy kingdom come" is the prayer of every Christian who intercedes for a lost friend or loved one. You are asking God to turn hearts to Him. Often when I ask God to save a lost person, I pray, "Thy kingdom come in his/her life."

I once had an opportunity to teach a seminar on fasting to Central Baptist Church in Chattanooga, Tennessee, in 1998 (the church is called Abba's House today). Pastor Ron Phillips organized 120 people in his church to fast during the month of November. At least one person fasted for each day of the month, and two or three people fasted for each Sunday and Wednesday. Some days there were as many as six people fasting and praying for evangelism. I came before the fast began to help them prepare to fast biblically and effectively.

The church was fasting in preparation for the annual Christmas musical called *The Book*, which tells the story of lost people appearing before God at the White Throne Judgment. Originally, the church planned a six-night run of the program. But so many people were converted that the play was extended for a total of 14 performances. A total of 998 people prayed to receive Christ. One evening alone, 153 people were converted. The revival got more than decisions to follow Christ. The church's Sunday school increased by 500 people each Sunday. The church service grew by 1,000 and offerings for the month of December went up $550,000 over the previous year. Plus, that year had an all-time record of baptisms. When you pray, "Thy kingdom come," the good news changes people's lives.

You can also pray, "Thy kingdom come," as you intercede for missionaries around the world. You're asking for the gospel to be proclaimed across every nation. The hymn composer Isaac Watts described the expansion of God's kingdom like this:

Jesus shall reign where'er the sun
Does his successive journeys run;
His kingdom spreads from shore to shore,
Till moon shall wax and wane no more.[1]

When you pray, "Thy kingdom come," you're also praying for the return of Jesus Christ to establish His kingdom on earth. You recognize that Jesus is not yet Ruler of all nations, so you're asking Jesus to come rule on earth just as He rules heaven today. You are praying with the apostle John in the last chapter of the Bible: "Even so, come, Lord Jesus!" (Rev. 22:20, *KJV*). You are praying for that time when "the kingdoms of this world have become the kingdoms of our Lord and of His Christ, and He shall reign forever and ever" (Rev. 11:15, *NKJV*). Presidents, kings and parliaments will no longer rule on earth. There will be no more mayors, governors or traffic courts.

When that time comes, the persecution of the Jews by rulers like Pharaoh will cease. Rulers like Herod will no longer kill babies.

Rulers like Nebuchadnezzar will no longer imprison Israel. Rulers like the Caesars who put Paul in jail and threw Christians to the lions will be no more. Gone will be the Hitlers who exterminate Jews and the Joseph Stalins who martyr priests of the Russian Orthodox Church. Communists will no longer imprison Christians and jihadi terrorists will no longer bomb churches. All terror will cease and death will be no more. In addition to that, there will be no more racial prejudice, no hatred of any kind. Jesus will reign over the earth.

Pray for Revival

"Thy kingdom come" is more than a prayer for evangelism and for the Second Coming. It is a prayer for revival among God's people on earth. Revival is when God pours out His Spirit on His people and empowers them to expand His kingdom. When you pray, "Thy kingdom come," you're asking God to rule your life on earth just as He rules heaven. The problem is, many who call themselves Christians reject His rule and do not follow Christ. Other Christians give God only half their time and resources. They go to church once in a while, give some money to good causes, and even do a few things to serve others. The problem is, God wants to rule our whole life, and He wants to do it here and now. God wants to rule us just as He rules in heaven. When more and more people submit their lives to His rule—that's revival.

What do you want from God when you pray, "Thy kingdom come"? Some people going through the agony of a terrible disease might pray, "Thy kingdom come," because they want God to give them a quick and painless death and for Jesus to receive them into heaven. God can use it to start a revival.

Some people pray, "Thy kingdom come," because they face a tense job situation or miserable family conditions. They pray, "Thy kingdom come," because they want some peace and joy on this earth. God can use it to start a revival.

Some people pray, "Thy kingdom come," because they want a second chance in life. They have messed up their family through divorce. Maybe they've scarred their life through an addictive habit and lost the asset of their strength or beauty. They want a "born-again" opportunity to start anew. And that's all right, because the Father is the God of the second chance. He can use it to start a revival.

Perhaps some pray, "Thy kingdom come," because they are enslaved to sin. They don't control their life, cigarettes do—or alcohol, or drugs or pornography. They can't say yes to God, only to sin. When they pray, "Thy kingdom come," they are asking God to liberate them and to rule in their life. And He can use it to start a revival.

Perhaps there are many people in jail who pray, "Thy kingdom come." They don't have freedom to go where they want, do what they want or even be what they want. There are millions behind bars in the United States and all over the world. They pray, "Thy kingdom come," and mean, "God, come into my cell and give me peace. Show me how to live in Your freedom." God can use it to start a revival.

Perhaps a Sunday School teacher walks into the classroom and prays, "Thy kingdom come," asking for God's presence to capture the hearts of the students, perhaps even change their lives. He wants God's kingdom to rule his teaching, to invade the lives of his students and transform them into dedicated followers of Jesus. That morning can be the start of a revival.

And then there's the business owner who prays, "Thy kingdom come." She jumps through government hoops and endures the strain of deadlines, meager profits and quarrelsome employees. When she prays, "Thy kingdom come, " she is asking God to take control of her business and direct her vocation in an abundant way. God can use it to start a marketplace revival.

Then there's the mother who desires to acknowledge the lordship of Christ in her life. When she prays, "Thy kingdom come," she is asking for God to use her motherly love for His glory. She's asking to be a better Christ-follower and a better mother with the help of the Holy Spirit. God can use families to start a revival.

Children can pray, "Thy kingdom come." Some people think this prayer is not appropriate for children because young ones are not yet mature enough to make life-changing choices. But Jesus said, "Let the little children come unto Me, and do not forbid them" (Matt. 19:14, *NKJV*). Even the youngest children can begin a habit of letting Jesus rule in their lives. God can use their innocence and devotion to start a revival.

And the aged can pray, "Thy kingdom come," because they have influence that can be used for God. Paul exhorts the "aged men" and "aged women" (Titus 2:2-3, *KJV*), indicating that God can use them in a powerful way in the lives of younger people. "Thy kingdom come . . . through my influence, example and desire to serve you." God can use people of any age to start a revival.

You may pray, "Thy kingdom come," for any one of a thousand reasons. God can use it to start a revival. Are you ready?

God's Rule in Your Life

How do we say yes to God's rule over our lives? First, we submit to the rule of grace, realizing that God has given us the exact opposite of what we deserve. Second, we submit to the indwelling Christ to rule us according to His will. Third, we submit to the rule of the Holy Spirit, allowing Him to guide and direct us in all we do. Fourth, we follow God's rule of love by which we relate to everyone. Finally, we learn His Word and apply it to our life, following its precepts and wisdom in deeds and actions.

It's important that we pray daily, "Thy kingdom come," because so often we are like the children of Israel: We accept God's forgiveness and enjoy being delivered from evil. But the freedom we enjoy is not acted out in our feet. God delivered Israel from the tyranny of Egypt and led them toward the Promised Land. But when they came to Kadesh-Barnea, the spies brought back a report that led Israel to believe they couldn't conquer the land God had promised (see Num. 13–14). The people rebelled in fear and unbelief; they didn't believe God could conquer the Promised Land—even after all He had already done! It was more than unbelief. It was a rejection of God's rule over their lives.

Another generation of Israelites conquered the Promised Land, but succeeding generations turned away from God. They demanded a king like the nations around them. They rejected God's rule when they demanded, "Now make us a king to judge us like all the nations" (1 Sam. 8:5, *NKJV*). God understood their hearts. He saw their intent. "But they have rejected Me, that I should not reign over them" (1 Sam. 8:7, *NKJV*).

When you pray, "Thy kingdom come," are you ready and willing to follow God's rule in your life?

Jesus does not yet have an earthly kingdom. He does not sit on a throne in Jerusalem or behind a desk in the Oval Office. Yet God's kingdom has come and is even now expanding—as it will until the final day when Christ comes again to make His rule on earth complete. Until then, Jesus wants to sit upon the throne of our hearts. When His followers do the will of God, they are able to win the lost to Jesus Christ and His kingdom expands. When Jesus' followers obey His Word, they are able to influence the world for righteousness and His kingdom expands.

Someday, every knee will bow and every tongue confess that Christ is Lord (see Phil. 2:9-11). Until then, confess with the apostle Paul Christ's kingship of your life: "Now to the King eternal, immortal, invisible, to God who alone is wise, be honor and glory forever and ever. Amen" (1 Tim. 1:17, *NKJV*).

Note

1. Isaac Watts, "Jesus Shall Reign," 1719. http://www.cyberhymnal.org/htm/j/s/jsreign.htm (accessed February 2013).

8

Third Petition: Thy Will Be Done

In the summer of 1951 I worked at Ben Lippin Camp, high in the mountains above Asheville, North Carolina. I and two other boys were hired to spend a week cleaning all of the winter muck out of the cabins, swimming pool, dining hall and lodge. One night around 9 o'clock, I was mopping the dining room floor and complaining to myself that my two buddies had gone to bed and left me holding the mop. I mopped myself over to a blue sign with silver letters that hung from a post in the middle of the dining room. It said, "God has a plan for your life."

I laughed at the sign and thought, *Is God's plan for me to do this job by myself and let my buddies slack off and go to sleep?* Suddenly the Spirit of God came over me, and I realized it *was* God's will for me to wash the dining room floor and to do the best job that could be done. I put my chin on the end of that mop handle and treated it like an old-fashioned altar. I surrendered my life to God, water pooling around my feet. I prayed, "Lord, I surrender my life to Your plan. Show me what You want me to do, and I will do it." I believe

God heard that simple prayer. I've made it a point, in the years since then, to pray it again each morning, reminding myself to surrender to His plan.

If you have not yet surrendered to God's will once and for all, I challenge you to pray, "Lord, show me Your plan for my life. I will do what You show me to do. I will be Your servant." Then remind yourself each day of your commitment by praying, "Your will be done in my life today."

Will to Do His Will

God knows what He wants us to do on this earth, and He leads those who are surrendered to Him. But many times we don't do what God wants us to do. Why? Perhaps we don't know God's will. Maybe we are fighting or rebelling against His will. By praying, "Thy will be done," we are asking God to show us His will and strengthen us to do it.

It has been said, "It's not the will to win that matters; everyone has that. It's the will to prepare to win that matters."[1] Winning begins with the will, when an athlete decides to do the hard work necessary to prepare to win. He or she sets aside other desires and focuses every energy on attaining the goal. Is God's will so important to you that you will set aside everything else in order to do it?

Sir Edmund Hillary and Tenzing Norgay were the first men to climb to the peak of Mount Everest. At first, Hillary, a New Zealander, saw Everest as an unconquerable goal. Even still, he decided to climb to the top. And so he began to prepare. In conversations with a friend of mine, James Davis, Hillary said he had many temptations that might have pulled him away from the challenge. But he remained focused on his goal. He also mentioned to James that there is a season when time and energy work either for you or against you, so he did his best to climb at the right time, at the peak of his physical energy.[2] Like Hillary, we have to know our seasons.

About his expedition to the South Pole several years later, he said, "While I was crossing Antarctica, I saw a glacier in a valley and I said to myself, *Climb down this valley, crawl across the glacier and climb to see what is on the other side of the mountain. Yet, I am young and have plenty of time to do this.*"[3] The far side of a glacial mountain was not what Hillary went to Antarctica to see. As tempting as it was, that mountain was not the goal. There's a lesson here. When pressing toward the goal, we must not let anything sidetrack what we intend to do.

Before he died in January 2008, Hillary had an experience with God. He sent word through my friend James inviting me to drop by and have tea with him. He had read my book *Fasting for a Spiritual Breakthrough*, and wanted to talk with me about conquering the most unconquerable thing in life: oneself.

Davis and I made plans to visit Hillary the last week of August 2007. But then I was asked to teach a class of doctoral students at Liberty University, so I put off the trip. The legendary mountaineer died just a few months later. If I hadn't let a class sidetrack me, I could have had tea with Sir Edmund Hillary! I must learn—as you also must learn—not to be sidetracked. We need the dedication of the apostle Paul, who wrote, "I once thought these things were valuable . . . but I focus on this one thing: Forgetting the past . . . I press on to reach the end of the race and receive the heavenly prize for which God, through Christ Jesus, is calling us" (Phil. 3:7,13-14, *NLT*).

What Is God's Will?

There are different expressions of God's will in various spheres of life. God has a will for the universe, which we see in the laws of nature such as gravity or the conservation of energy. God created the world (see John 1:3) and God keeps the world running (see Col. 1:17). It is God's will that the universe work in certain ways, and we see His will at work as we observe the natural world.

God has physical laws for humans, which we can understand by observing how our bodies function best. These laws are God's will for how to care for our bodies. We are to breathe, eat and exercise each day. We must protect ourselves against becoming too cold or too hot, and from germs, disease and physical harm. We must rest and sleep. By caring for God's gift of a body, we honor Him.

God has a will concerning evangelism and how His work is done. "The Lord is not slow in keeping his promise, as some understand slowness. Instead he is patient . . . not wanting anyone to perish, but everyone to come to repentance" (2 Pet. 3:9). God uses many means, including dedicated believers and "the foolishness of preaching" (1 Cor. 1:21, *KJV*) to win lost people to Himself. Because evangelism is God's will, Paul said, "Woe is me if I do not preach the gospel!" (1 Cor. 9:16, *NKJV*).

God wills for each Christian to grow mature. Each believer must yield his life to Christ (see Rom. 12:1), then read and learn the Bible to grow in Christ (see 2 Pet. 3:18). He must pray daily (see 1 Thess. 5:17) and worship both privately (see Matt. 6:6) and with other believers (see Col. 3:16). He must fellowship with other believers in a church (see Heb. 10:25) and give tithes and offerings to God (see Mal. 3:10; 1 Cor. 16:1-2). Christians must witness to the lost (see Matt. 28:19-20) and serve the Lord by serving others (see Matt. 25:31-46).

God wills for every believer to serve the Church and the world. Each Christian receives spiritual gifts that empower her to carry out His plan on earth. To one person, God gives the gift of prophecy so he can preach. To another God gives the gift of teaching so she can pass on knowledge to those who need it. To another God gives the gift of mercy so he can help others cope with their difficulties and problems of life. And still others have the gift of giving . . . or evangelism . . . or administration . . . or leadership.[4]

When you pray, "Thy will be done," you are praying for God to use you, your spiritual gifts and your earthly resources to accomplish His will for you and for others. You're asking God to have His way in your life.

And you don't do it only once. Doing God's will is akin to being married. Of course, the wedding—the day you surrender your life to God's plan—is the "yes" that starts it all. But as every happily married couple will tell you, that "yes" has to be said every single day if the relationship will last! Likewise, each and every day you must surrender anew to God's will for your life.

"Thy will be done on earth as it is in heaven." Begin with yourself. Pray that you will find and do God's will today. And then pray the same tomorrow.

Fasting is one of the most practical ways of surrendering your life to God's will. It's one thing to want to surrender your inner person to God, but when you surrender your appetite, it's a whole different ball game. Each time you miss a meal, you are searching for God's will in your life. So fast and pray, "Thy will be done."

Notes

1. This quote has been variously attributed to Vince Lombardi, Bear Bryant and Bobby Knight. They may have all said one version or another of this sentiment.
2. This is quoted material based on conversations in 2007 between Sir Edmund Hillary and James O. Davis, founder of Cutting Edge International and cofounder of Billion Soul Network. Incidents and conversations verified by James O. Davis by email, March 6, 2013.
3. Ibid.
4. For a Spiritual Gifts Inventory to help find your spiritual gifts, visit http://elmertowns.com/spiritual_gifts_test/.

9

Fourth Petition: Give Us Our Daily Bread

Twenty years ago I was teaching the Lord's Prayer in the Pastor's Bible Class at my church. A bald-headed salesman came up to me on the platform, which was unusual; lay people in our church didn't often venture behind the pulpit. But what really caught my attention was the hat he was wearing in church. Times may have changed, but back then wearing a hat in church was considered the height of disrespect. Before I could ask him to remove it, he said, "My hat is on because I want to show you something."

He told the class that he worked for a local Sears department store selling appliances. He was in the upper bracket of sales and had, on several occasions, achieved the best sales record in the store. Then he pointed to his head and said that his hat had everything to do with his success.

At work, he dressed in a white shirt and tie and always wore the hat. "Most people think I wear this hat because I'm bald, but that's not it," he said. He explained that after making his best sales pitch, there came a time in every presentation when he would press for a decision. For years, his fellow workers had watched him remove his hat at that point in the presentation and thought it was magic. "There he goes again, taking off his hat. He'll get this sale for sure."

But it wasn't magic. "At that moment, I take off my hat and see the small printed card under the inner band that reads, 'Give us this day our daily bread.'" He went on to explain that he needed his sales commission to feed his family, pay the rent and put his three kids through college. His commissions were his "daily bread." And so, as potential customers weighed their decisions, the salesman took off his hat and prayed for God to provide.

Bread of Life

Think about the wide variety of bread choices we have available in our supermarkets. There is white bread, whole-wheat bread, multigrain bread, dinner rolls, hamburger rolls, sweet rolls, hot dog buns. You can get bread in any size, in any shape and at almost any price. Some bread is frozen, ready to cook. Some stores have day-old bread at a discount. There may be a few older folks around who remember when you brought your loaf home and sliced it yourself, but nowadays sliced bread it just the norm.

Bread is so plentiful and convenient that many Americans take it for granted. Is it the same around the world? No. More than 870 million people across the globe do not have access to enough food.[1] For them, the need for daily bread is literal. Imagine you have not had any bread, or anything else to eat, for three or four days. Imagine you're very hungry—so hungry that you have never in your life felt full. When you pray, "Give us our daily bread," your petition is offered with urgency and desperation.

Perhaps those of us who have more than enough need to pray this prayer on behalf of those who don't. When next you pray the Lord's Prayer, set aside a few minutes to intercede for those around the world who don't know how they will feed their children. When you're fasting is a good time to intercede in this way. You are feeling in your own body, in a lesser way, what it is like to be hungry. You can empathize with those who feel pangs of hunger on a daily basis.

Most people reading this book are not starving. They don't have to pray for bread. Most Americans have a job, and the majority who don't have access to food stamps or the opportunity to live with extended family who can help to provide for their needs. If anything, most Americans ought to pray, "Lord, thank You for bread," rather than asking for it.

But what about spiritual bread? Is America starving for spiritual food? Are you?

Jesus said, "I am the bread of life. He who comes to Me shall never hunger, and he who believes in Me shall never thirst" (John 6:35, *NKJV*). It can be difficult, when you are just getting started with fasting, to focus on anything besides your physical hunger. The empty feeling in your stomach is distracting. You may fantasize about your favorite foods.

I love egg salad sandwiches. I just feel satisfied when I bite, chew and swallow. Perhaps I'm remembering my childhood; we kept chickens in the backyard and when money was short, Mother would send me to gather eggs. We'd hard boil them and enjoy fresh egg salad. In August Mother would send me to our garden to pick tomatoes. We'd slice them thick, toast some bread and swipe butter on one slice and mayo on the other. Mother convinced me we ate better than the rich because our food was fresher.

My mouth is watering just thinking about it! And that's what it's like in the early days of fasting—so prepare yourself. But as you practice fasting and learn to turn your focus away from what you're giving up—like egg salad sandwiches—toward Christ, the hunger that has gnawed the pit of your spirit begins to be satisfied.

The psalmist wrote, "Oh, taste and see that the Lord is good; blessed is the man who trusts in Him!" (Ps. 34:8, *NKJV*). Jesus said:

> I tell you the truth, anyone who believes has eternal life. Yes, I am the bread of life! Your ancestors ate manna in the wilderness, but they all died. Anyone who eats the bread from heaven, however, will never die. I am the living bread that came down from heaven. Anyone who eats this bread will live forever; and this bread, which I will offer so the world may live, is my flesh (John 6:47-51, *NLT*).

When you eat an egg salad sandwich, it becomes a part of you. Food gives you physical strength to continue living. But when you fast and pray, when you study the Word of God and meditate on His goodness, then the Father satisfies your longing for relationship with Him. You feast on His Word and presence, and they become a part of you. Withholding food gives you spiritual strength to continue living.

Notice, in the Lord's Prayer, the request for *daily* bread. Have you ever wondered why God created us with daily needs? Our body gets hungry every day and we need food to satisfy it. Maybe God created us that way so we wouldn't stray too far from Him. We turn to God to meet our daily physical needs, just as the Sears appliance salesman did. But we also understand that only fellowship with God can satisfy our spiritual hunger, and we turn to God daily to meet that need as well. By fasting, we give up pursuit of the first need to focus on the second.

Following Christ is a sacrifice. When Jesus calls us, He challenges, "If any of you wants to be my follower, you must turn from your selfish ways, take up your cross daily, and follow me" (Luke 9:23, *NLT*). On another occasion Jesus said, "You cannot become my disciple without giving up everything you own" (Luke 14:33,

NLT). Jesus did not make it easy to follow Him. But consider Peter and Andrew, who gave up fishing to follow Jesus. When they were with Jesus, do you think they sat around wishing for their old lives back? When Matthew walked just a few steps behind Jesus, do you think he wanted to go back to the old IRS tax counter? Do you really think the other disciples yearned for the good old days, before the Messiah came into their lives?

If you focus too much on physical bread, all you'll get is physical hunger. But if you focus primarily on the Bread of Life, you will find soul satisfaction.

Asking for Things

When you pray, "Give us our daily bread," you are asking for more than bread. Yes, this petition includes food that gives us strength to live. It also includes other things we need, such as transportation to work, clothes to keep warm and a roof over our heads. Bread symbolizes all the needs of our life, including food.

But this petition is also the only place in the Lord's Prayer where we ask for things. We may ask for healing, a job, guidance in a difficult relationship or money for college tuition. We may ask for pots to cook the food God provides, a computer to communicate with friends or a cell phone to keep in touch with family. We may ask for things that are not necessities but might bring joy to our life, such as a family vacation, sports equipment or an iPhone that can do just about anything.

I learned to ask for things in my first semester of college. As a 17-year-old freshman, I began to pray for the things I needed—including money. And God answered my request. I wrote a personal letter to each of my aunts and uncles, telling them of my conversion and asking them to accept Christ as Savior. In response, some sent me small checks of around $10 each. I paid all of my expenses that year . . . barely. And I learned that God answers prayer, if only I would ask Him.

Here are a few things I learned about asking God for things.

1. Pray Specifically

Make a specific request for what you want God to provide. Yes, you can start, "Give us this day our daily bread," but go beyond that to ask for the specific thing you want. James tells us, "Ye have not, because ye ask not" (Jas. 4:2, *KJV*).

God wants you to pray for specific things. That's why Jesus said, "If you ask anything in My name, I will do it" (John 14:14, *NKJV*). Pray for big things and pray for little things. Why? Because when you ask for big things, God is honored by your recognition that He is able to do big things. And when you ask for little things, you establish a trust relationship with Him to provide your everyday needs and desires of life.

But remember, you will not get everything you request in prayer. You *will* have unanswered prayers. Even the great apostle Paul prayed for some things he didn't get. "Three different times I begged the Lord to take it away" (that is, his thorn in the flesh). "Each time he said, 'My gracious favor is all you need. My power works best in weakness'" (2 Cor. 12:8-9, *NLT*).

2. Pray According to the Will of God

You will receive a greater number of answered prayers if you pray according to the will of God. Notice that the petition "Thy will be done on earth as it is in heaven" precedes the petition for God to meet your needs. There's a good reason for this: It helps us remember that God's will is far more important than any request we bring to Him.

John tells us, "And we are confident that he hears us whenever we ask for anything that pleases him" (1 John 5:14, *NLT*). This verse promises that God will listen to us; it doesn't promise that He will answer the way we hope He will. Even yielded Christians may ask God for things that are not consistent with His will. Some are blinded by their circumstances or by their limited point of view—no one but God can see the impact, both negative and positive, of an answered prayer.

Others are deceived by their desires. They can't see past their hopes and dreams to God's will, so they pray wrongly. In the mid '70s, a college-age couple told me early before a morning class that they had run off across state lines the previous weekend to get married. I counseled them to tell their parents immediately after class. Later that same morning, a love-struck young man told me that he felt it was God's will for him to marry the girl who had just gotten married. (She was cute, vivacious and a spiritual go-getter, and I didn't blame him.) I was tempted to laugh in the face of the passionate young man; clearly, it was not God's will for him to marry her! Because the newly wedded couple hadn't even shared with their parents, I couldn't yet tell the poor young man that the girl was already married. All I could do was ask questions about his ability to know God's will.

We get answers to prayer when we pray according to God's will. We find the will of God in the Word of God, so study and meditation on Scripture are key components in a prayer life that is in line with God's will.

3. Pray According to Scripture

Pray under the guidance of Scripture. Jesus said, "If you remain in me and my words remain in you, you may ask for anything you want, and it will be granted!" (John 15:7, *NLT*). The key here is remaining in Jesus. Rock-and-roll icon Janice Joplin sang, "O Lord, won't you buy me a Mercedes-Benz? All my friends drive Porsches!"[2] Now, if Janice had been in close fellowship with Jesus, she'd have known that request was outlandish! When you remain in Christ and search out His Word for wisdom, you will find your request for a new Cadillac or Rolls Royce, or an ocean-view luxury penthouse, falling to the bottom of your prayer list.

Maybe God can't trust you with money; if you had an unlimited bank account, you wouldn't trust Him to supply your daily needs. Maybe God keeps you on a short financial leash to keep you in fellowship with Him. When you pray according to Scripture's wisdom, you don't ask for things that would come between you and the Lord. Learn God's Word. Hide it in your heart so you do not sin (see Ps. 119:11).

4. Pray Obediently

God answers the prayers of those who obey Him. "We will receive from him whatever we ask because we obey him and do the things that please him" (1 John 3:22, *NLT*). How does God look on the requests of one who seldom attends church, doesn't worship Him with other believers and doesn't offer tithes and offerings to Him? Of course, just because you don't have good fellowship with your church doesn't mean you have broken fellowship with the Lord. But often, fellowship with one is symptomatic of fellowship with the other. Isn't the church called the Body of Christ (see Eph. 1:22-23), and doesn't Christ love the church (see Eph. 5:25)? Jesus' followers are commanded to worship together (see Heb. 10:25). Your obedience in this area could determine whether your prayers will be answered.

There are other areas of life in which obedience may impact the effectiveness of our prayers. Family, for instance. Children should obey their parents (see Eph. 6:1). A wife should submit to her husband (see Eph. 5:22). A husband should love his wife (see Eph. 5:25) and submit to her (see Eph. 5:21).

Or, for another example, our relationships with others. We must love our neighbors (see Matt. 22:39; Luke 10:25-37). We must forgive those who sin against us (see Mark 11:25-26). We must love all people (see Rom. 13:8-10). We must obey our government (see Rom. 13) and pray for our political leaders (see 1 Tim. 2:1-2).

When you consider all the directives for believers, you come to the realization that it's impossible to be a perfect Christian! Hence, it's impossible to be perfectly obedient in order that our prayers are always answered. But remember, when we pray to the Father through Jesus, we do not come to the throne alone. We come in the company of the One who was obedient even unto death on a cross (see Phil. 2:4-8). We are called to obedience, but even when we are not perfect the Father hears our prayers because of the Son's sacrifice on our behalf.

5. Pray Persistently

Pray continually and with perseverance. Jesus said, "Keep on asking, and you will receive what you ask for. Keep on seeking, and you will find. Keep on knocking, and the door will be opened" (Matt. 7:7, *NLT*). Persistence is not begging; the one who continually begs is trying to wear down the resistance of the giver. You can't do that to God, because God will not change (see Mal. 3:6). We keep asking in faith, knowing God will answer if and when it is His will. And we keep asking because there may be reasons God delays sending an answer:

- It takes time to get an answer to you.
- The answer you seek may not exist yet.
- You need to learn lessons before God answers.
- Other people are not yet ready to be involved.
- God has a better way of answering.
- Your requested answer may hurt others.
- Circumstances are not right.

It may be that God begins to answer your request, but as He is working out details behind the scenes, you give up and quit praying.

Not only that, you forget about your request and move on to another area of your life. You don't even care about the answer anymore. If that happens, wouldn't it be logical for God to stop the process of answering that prayer? Because you quit asking, God quit answering.

A discouraged Elijah prayed several times to die, but then God gave him a new task (see 1 Kings 19). Picture Elijah praying to die, but God responding, "No! I have a better idea." God planned for Elijah to enter heaven in a chariot of fire with a whirlwind (see 2 Kings 2:11-12). That sounds a lot better than having to die! Sometimes you pray for one thing and God gives you something better.

6. Ask Because You Serve the Lord

Fruit-bearing is Jesus' next condition for answers to prayer: "I chose you. I appointed you to go and produce lasting fruit, so that the Father will give you whatever you ask for, using my name" (John 15:16, *NLT*). What a promise! As we bear fruit, the Father answers our prayers. We are chosen by Jesus to produce fruit (the first part is His command), and He promises, in response to that fruit, to give anything we ask in His name (the second part is His blessing).

Have you asked God to help you produce fruit in the Sunday school class you teach? Perhaps God uses your lessons to the extent of your preparation and prayer. Consider this equation: *Little prayer = little power. More prayer = more power. Much prayer = much power.* How much prayer are you pouring over your class? Have you prayed for a long time, with tears, for the lives of your class members to be transformed?

Fast to Feed Your Soul

What bread (food) does for you physically, fasting does for you spiritually. Bread gives you energy to work and vitality to live. Likewise, putting first the Bread of Life by fasting energizes and vitalizes your spirit to love and serve God and work to expand His kingdom.

Bread keeps you from becoming mentally sluggish. When you begin to get hungry, your growling stomach becomes a distraction from the mental tasks you'd like to accomplish. You may be surprised to find that, like physical food, fasting brings mental and spiritual clarity. Once when I was coming to the end of a 40-day fast, I was amazed at my mental sharpness. Rather than feeling tired and sluggish, I found greater insight and inspiration to preach and write. Then a doctor told me that, when you're not eating, your digestive system is not working very hard and so needs less blood circulated to its organs. Now all that extra oxygen-rich blood is available to your brain. More blood to the brain makes you think better. Once the initial hunger pangs subside, fasting brings mental and spiritual focus.

Bread helps you stay emotionally balanced. When you haven't had enough to eat, you probably have a tendency to get irritable and easily upset. When you're well fed, it's easier to be positive and loving toward others. So why would giving up food lead to greater emotional balance? Because you put the Bread of Life on the throne of your heart, where the Spirit's presence begins to shape your character like Christ's. Your ability to feel and show love, joy, peace, patience, kindness, goodness, faithfulness, gentleness and self-control (see Gal. 5:22-23) does not depend on food but on the closeness you experience with God.

When you pray, "Give us our daily bread," you are asking God to provide for your needs—and your greatest need is for more of Him. Let the Bread of Life satisfy the hunger in your heart.

Notes

1. Food and Agricultural Organization of the United Nations, "Globally Almost 870 Million Chronically Undernourished—New Hunger Report," October 9, 2012. http://www.fao.org/news/story/en/item/161819/icode/ (accessed June 2013).
2. Janis Joplin, Michael McClure and Bob Neuwirth, "Mercedes Benz," 1970.

10

Fifth Petition: Forgive Us Our Debts

When Jesus taught His followers to pray the Lord's Prayer, He chose the perfect word to describe our sins: *debts.* We pray, "Forgive us our debts." A debt is an obligation we owe to creditors. Likewise, our debts are obligations we owe to God. When we ask for forgiveness of our debts, we are asking to return to fellowship with the Father.

Why does the Lord's Prayer use the Greek word for "debt" instead of "sins"? The Greek word for "sin" used most often in the New Testament means, literally, "to miss the mark." But Jesus did not tell us to pray, "Forgive us for missing the mark." Why? Because debts involve a relationship—a relationship that was established when you turned your life to Christ. We have been saved from our sins and adopted into the family of God. But when we sin, our fellowship with the Father is disrupted.

Think of Jesus' story of the son who demands his family inheritance before his father's death (see Luke 15:11-24). The prodigal is a picture of a hardened heart in rebellion against God. He cares nothing for the feelings of his father and turns his back on his family obligations. He walks away without looking back. By his own selfish choice, he has broken fellowship with his father.

Then everything goes wrong. His worldly friends take his money and walk away, just as he had walked away from his family. When an economic depression falls on the land, he ends up feeding hogs to scratch out a living—and in that pigpen, he loses what's left of his self-respect.

He recalls the father who had loved him so much and he feels ashamed of himself, not just because of his present shameful circumstances but also because of his selfishness and greed. But maybe things could be different. "When he finally came to his senses, he said to himself, 'At home even the hired servants have food enough to spare, and here I am dying of hunger! I will go home to my father and say, "Father, I have sinned against both heaven and you, and I am no longer worthy of being called your son. Please take me on as a hired servant"'" (Luke 15:18-19, *NLT*).

Father, I have sinned.

Forgive us our debts.

In Debt to the Father

Saying the words is not magic. What matters is your heart. "Godly sorrow produces repentance" (2 Cor. 7:10, *NKJV*). What is godly sorrow? Sorrow that leads to godliness! You are sorry to the depths of your heart, and you intend never to do it again. The Father watches for our repentance and return to Him, ready to wrap us in His embrace when we turn toward home.

When Christians pray, "Forgive us our debts," we are acknowledging that we sin, and that these sins have disrupted our fellowship with the Father. We are not begging for salvation; we are already children of God if we have received Christ as Savior and Lord. Rather, we are praying for parental forgiveness.

Imagine a mother has baked a batch of warm chocolate-chip cookies and left them on the kitchen counter to cool. She tells her sweet little girl, "Don't touch those cookies; they are for dessert."

You might think every sweet little girl would obey. But when the mother leaves the room and returns, one of the cookies is missing and her daughter's face and hands are smeared with chocolate. The mother asks, "Did you take a cookie?" The little girl shakes her head, "No!" But Mother knows better.

The Bible says, "If we claim we have not sin, we are only fooling ourselves and not living in the truth. . . . If we claim we have not sinned, we are calling God a liar and showing that his word has no place in our hearts" (1 John 1:8,10, *NLT*). A little girl taking a cookie and then lying about it might seem like an innocent thing, but the truth is that stealing and dishonesty disrupt the closeness of family relationships. The little girl is still her mother's daughter—nothing she can do will change that. But trust has been broken between them and will not return until the little girl repents.

Sometimes when we sin, we do what we shouldn't. Other times, we don't do what we should. Picture a father who instructs his teenage boy to fill up the family car with gas and then wash it inside and out before the family leaves on vacation. But the son gets busy playing video games or hanging out with friends and doesn't get around to obeying his father's instructions. The father will probably take care of the car so the family can leave on time, but you can bet he is grieved and upset by the son's disobedience. Fellowship between them has been broken because the son did not do what he should have done.

The boy disobeyed his father, but you can't say he is no longer a member of the family. There is still a physical relationship but the boy has broken fellowship with his father. The boy is still the son of his father, but he's a disobedient son.

That's a perfect image of our relationship to God. We are children of God if we are in Christ, but when we sin—whether by doing what we shouldn't or by not doing what we should—we are disobedient children. By our own selfish choice, our fellowship with the Father has been broken.

So we pray, "Forgive us our debts."

Forgive Your Debtors

You may have heard in Sunday school or church that God offers forgiveness freely, no strings attached. And it's true that "by grace you have been saved, through faith—and this is not from yourselves, it is the gift of God—not by works, so that no one can boast" (Eph. 2:8-9). Our salvation does not depend on anything we do, but on God's grace.

When it comes to debts that break our fellowship with the Father, however, the Bible is clear: We must forgive in order to be forgiven. Remember Jesus' parable of the unforgiving servant (see Matt. 18:21-35)? A certain servant owes the king 10,000 talents—an amount of money that, in the time of Jesus, was all but unimaginable. (If Jesus were telling the story today, He might say "a gazillion dollars" to have the same effect.) Instead of selling the servant and his family into slavery, however, the king has compassion on the servant and forgives the debt.

That same servant demands that another servant pay the 100 denarii owed to him (one denarius was considered a fair day's wage). But when the other servant can't pay, he has the debtor thrown into prison. When the king finds out, he is angry: "You evil servant! I forgave you that tremendous debt because you pleaded with me. Shouldn't you have mercy on your fellow servant, just as I had mercy on you?" (Matt. 18:32-33, *NLT*). And the king hands over the unforgiving servant to prison to be tortured until he can somehow pay his unpayable debt.

Jesus ended the parable with this warning: "That's what my heavenly Father will do to you if you refuse to forgive your brothers and sisters from your heart" (Matt. 18:35, *NLT*). A stern warning, indeed.

Why was Jesus so emphatic about the need to forgive our debtors? Because unforgiveness breaks our fellowship with others *and* with the Father. It runs completely counter to the Great Commandment. Jesus said, "'Love the Lord your God with all your heart and with all your soul and with all your mind.' This is the first and greatest commandment. And the second is like it: 'Love your neighbor as yourself'" (Matt. 22:37-39). The Greek phrase translated here as "the second is like it" evokes the idea of a mirror image. Jesus was saying that obeying the commandment to love your neighbor is a reflection of your obedience to the commandment to love God. If you love God, you will love your neighbor. And that means offering forgiveness when he or she sins against you.

When you pray, "Forgive us our debts," don't forget also to pray, "as we forgive our debtors." Jesus said, "When you stand praying, if you hold anything against anyone, forgive them, so that your Father in heaven may forgive you your sins" (Mark 11:25). Before you move on to the next petition of the Lord's Prayer, forgive your brother's debt. Forgive your sister's debt.

The Father will be overjoyed to welcome all of you home.

Fasting Against Sin

Fasting is a spiritual discipline—that is, a way of training the spirit to hear and respond to God. One reason spiritual disciplines such as fasting are so effective is that we are less likely to do (or not do) something to break our fellowship with the Father when we're in wholehearted pursuit of Him.

We all sin, whether out of selfishness or even weakness. Paul admitted, "I don't want to do what is wrong, but I do it anyway" (Rom.

7:19, *NLT*). Pursuing God through prayer and fasting can help us break out of sinful patterns of behavior. We practice denying ourselves and seeking God in prayer—exactly what we should do when faced with temptation! Fasting exercises the spiritual muscles we need to turn away from sin and run toward God.

When you pray, "Forgive us our debts," you are acknowledging that you sin. When you fast, you are telling the Lord that you don't want to sin anymore.

Read on for more about fasting and resisting temptation . . .

11

Sixth Petition: Lead Us Not into Temptation

In the last chapter, you learned to ask forgiveness for past sins by praying, "Forgive us our debts." When you pray, "Lead us not into temptation," you are asking God to protect you from future sins. This petition focuses on potential sins, while the previous petition focuses on actual sins. When God answers both prayers, you are delivered from both your past sins and future temptations.

The sixth petition recognizes that God is your leader through life. Remember the beloved Twenty-third Psalm? "The Lord is my shepherd, I shall not want. . . . He leadeth me beside still waters . . ." (vv. 1-2, *KJV*). You are asking Him to lead you on a path far from temptation. In one sense, it's probably impossible for the Lord to lead you where there is not temptation. Why? Because temptation is found in almost every place, almost all the time. Notice that Jesus did not teach His followers to pray, "Lead us not *by* temptation," or "Lead us not *around* temptation," or "Lead us not *over* temptation."

No, He instructed us to pray, "Lead us not *into* temptation." Why? Because temptation is an unavoidable reality that God can lead you by, around and over. But the inevitability of temptation doesn't mean you need to get in the thick of it! *Into* temptation implies smack in the middle, where you are surrounded and don't see an immediate escape. So really you are saying, "Lord, don't let me be overwhelmed by temptation."

You're not praying, "Lord, don't tempt me." God will never lead you to sin. He is holy and good. He cannot sin, nor will He ever tempt you to sin. The Bible says it this way: "Let no man say when he is tempted, I am tempted of God: for God cannot be tempted with evil, neither tempteth he any man" (Jas. 1:13, *KJV*).

You're not praying, "Don't let me be tempted," for that is asking to live in a world that does not exist. Our culture is rife with every kind of temptation: to cheat a little to get ahead, to eat more than our body needs, to visit an online porn site, to idolize celebrities and sports stars, to ignore those in need to keep more for ourselves. But the reality of temptation does not give us an excuse to sin.

Neither does ignorance give us an excuse. Think about a small child standing on the sidewalk across the street from a playground. Suddenly, another child's ball bounces out of the playground and into the street. The toddler on the far sidewalk sees the ball and is tempted to run and get it—right into oncoming traffic. His eyes are on the ball, not on the dangers that surround him. His wise daddy, however, sees both the ball and the traffic, and reaches for the toddler's hand to stop his suicidal dash.

Sometimes we are like that small child: ignorant of the dangers that surround us. All we can see is the thing we want, not the consequences of pursuing it. But when we feel the Father's restraining hand—through His Word, the warning of a godly friend, the nudge of the Holy Spirit on our mind—we must obey or face the consequences of our disobedience.

When you pray, "Lead us not into temptation," it is the cry of one who has drunk the bitter dregs of sin and does not want to taste them again. You know from painful experience that sin has consequences, and you don't want to hurt or be hurt again. This is not a head prayer that only thinks in abstract concepts. It is a heart prayer that feels dread and desperation to avoid sin at all costs.

Love Not the World

There is within each of us a Dr. Jekyll and a Mr. Hyde. One is the redeemed, restored person who desires to turn his face continually toward God. The other is the sin nature that pulls him toward destruction. When you pray, "Lead us not into temptation," you are asking God to help you be and act as the regenerated child of God you are and win victory over your sin nature.

When we turn habitually to our sin nature, we eventually become habitual sinners. Sin makes us into addicts, and we become slaves to alcohol or drugs, to pornography or food, to greed or rage. Sin is a tyrannical master that abuses and traumatizes. It makes us forget our desire to live a good, loving, God-pleasing life. It makes us lose our self-control, our temper and our dignity. And when we give ourselves continually to sin, we lose our friends, our jobs and our marriages.

The Evil One and his forces have set a trap to ensnare believers—a trap that will entice and persuade if we do not stay on our guard. What is the trap? "Love not the world, neither the things that are in the world . . . for all that is in the world, the lust of the flesh, and the lust of the eyes, and the pride of life, is not of the Father, but is of the world" (1 John 2:15-16, *KJV*). When the Bible uses the term "world," it is not referring to beautiful things in God's creation such as purple mountains, meandering streams and ocean waves lapping against a pristine beach. No, the "world" means a system of values that is contrary to God's will. The world system tells us we should gratify our desire for pleasure (the lust of the flesh), our craving for ever more material things (the lust of the eyes), and our longing to feel superior to everyone else (the pride of life). But these are not God's values.

God's values are enshrined in the Ten Commandments, the moral code of the universe. When someone ignores or rejects the Ten Commandments, she has fallen into Satan's trap. She wants to go her own way, to do her own thing, to fulfill her own desires. She is ensnared by the world system, and it is just a matter of time until her habitual sinning leads to painful or even deadly consequences.

When you pray, "Lead us not into temptation," you are asking God to keep you from falling into the Enemy's snare. You are asking Him to give you strength to live by His values, not the values of the world.

Is it the end of the world if you slip up and sin one time? No. John tells us, "If we confess our sins, He is faithful and just to forgive us our sins and to cleanse us from all unrighteousness" (1 John 1:9, *KJV*). Don't become neurotic over the Enemy's attacks on you. Don't get obsessed if you sin on occasion. Instead, get your eyes off of sin and focus your eyes on Jesus. He has already won the victory over sin and death. When you pray, "Lead us not into temptation," you recognize that the Holy Spirit wants to enable you to obey God and bring honor to the Lord Jesus Christ. You recognize that you can resist temptation and bring glory to God through a life of victory over sin.

Temptation Can Strengthen Your Faith

God allows us to face trials and temptations to test and strengthen our faith. But He never allows us to be tempted beyond what we can resist. Paul wrote, "God is faithful. He will not allow the temptation to be more than you can stand. When you are tempted, he will show you a way out so that you can endure" (1 Cor. 10:13, *NLT*). God desires us to be victorious over sin, and will always provide a way to resist or escape temptation.

When you face temptation, you always have a choice. You can yield to temptation or to God's will. And the more often you choose God's will over sin, the stronger your faith will become. Every temptation you choose to resist or escape is training for your race toward God. It makes you stronger and increases your endurance.

When you pray, "Lead us not into temptation," you are recognizing the tests that lie ahead and asking God to help you endure. Life is like school: In order to progress, we must learn our lessons. And we find out if we've learned our lessons by being tested. In first grade, we were tested to see if we could print the letters of the alphabet. In the middle grades, we were tested to see if we could use letters to make words and sentences, perhaps even paragraphs. By the time we got into middle school, we were tested to see if we could write several short paragraphs. Before long, we turned paragraphs into term papers that were graded to assess our progress.

If we learned our lessons well, by the time we were in high school or college we were no longer threatened by the tests we passed in the first grade. And it is the same for the Christian life. Each new season offers to teach us lessons we must master in order to progress. And we are tested to ensure we are learning, growing and becoming more like Christ.

The tests, of course, get more difficult along the way. But every victory strengthens you for greater victory. If you win today over a small temptation, you are better prepared to win over the bigger temptation down the road. As you grow, your hurdles get higher and your challenges get harder. That is as it should be! The apostle James wrote, "Consider it pure joy, my brothers and sisters, whenever you face trials of many kinds, because you know that the testing of your faith produces perseverance. Let perseverance finish its work so that you may be mature and complete, not lacking anything" (Jas. 1:2-4).

The Test of Fasting

One way you can practice facing trials and tests with joy is by fasting. A fast is, in one sense, a trial or test that you choose for yourself in order to grow closer to God and get answers to your prayers. When you prepare food for your kids or smell your neighbor's baby back ribs slow-roasting on the grill, you will likely be tempted to break your fast. At such a moment, rejoice! Take joy in the knowledge that you are giving your spiritual muscles a workout so you can be stronger down the road.

Most of us need all the spiritual exercise we can get lest the devil's snares prove too great a temptation. When you fast and pray, "Lead us not into temptation," you are trusting that God will sustain you through a test you have chosen out of obedience to Him. This test, in turn, prepares you to reject the Enemy's schemes. You are praying for victory today so you can win the victory tomorrow.

Only trusting the Lord leads to victory. According to Romans 13, your mouth can't be trusted to keep you from speaking evil. Your feet can't be trusted to keep you from following after sin. Your eyes can't be trusted to keep you from looking for sin. Your mind can't be trusted to keep you from dwelling on sin. Your intentions can't be trusted to keep you from sinning. Victory over sin only comes by trusting the Lord. And your trust will deepen with every successful fast.

Fasting is also a test of your obedience. I call it "sanctified obedience," because the act of obeying causes you to grow in holiness. By fasting, you are setting yourself apart from sin by doing what Jesus commanded His disciples to do (see Matt. 6:16-17). When you fast and pray, "Lead us not into temptation," you are letting God know you're so serious about holiness that you are willing to set aside time, food and other necessities to seek more of it in your life.

When you fast and pray, "Lead us not into temptation," you are also asking God to show you the roots of your sin—that is, the unmet need or unacknowledged desire that lies behind the sins you are most drawn to commit. For instance, one man may struggle most with greed, wrestling with the temptation to hoard money rather than stewarding his resources as gifts from God. But another man struggles most with lust, wrestling with the temptation to view women as objects for his gratification rather than as image-bearers of God. The unconscious roots of greed and lust lie in different unmet needs—needs that God alone can meet. Fasting and praying, "Lead us not into temptation," is your invitation to the Holy Spirit to reveal the roots of your sin and to heal you.

Finally, a fast can actually be a part of God's answer to your prayer, "Lead us not into temptation." Let me illustrate with a story.

A young Christian man was sleeping with a young lady. He knew that having sex with her was a sin because they were not married. He knew it was wrong, but he really enjoyed it. He thought to himself, *How can something so good be sinful?*

He knew the Seventh Commandment: "Thou shalt not commit adultery" (Exod. 20:14). But he could not stop making trips to her house to do just that. He knew what Paul wrote: "Now the body is not for sexual immorality, but for the Lord" (1 Cor. 6:13, *NKJV*) and "Flee immorality . . . he who commits sexual immorality sins against his own body" (1 Cor. 6:18, *NKJV*). But he could not flee.

The young man decided to go on an extended fast to sort things out, and to pray the Lord's Prayer as part of his time with God. He even left town so he wouldn't contact his girlfriend while he fasted. While he was away, he found out she was pregnant—and that he was not the father. A friend of his had been keeping the girlfriend company behind his back.

In an instant, the young man knew God had answered his prayer. Any temptation for sex with her was immediately gone—and in its place was a deep desire to draw close to his heavenly Father, whose commands he had willfully ignored. God had led him away from temptation and into a closer relationship with Himself.

If you are struggling with a persistent temptation that continually overcomes your ability to resist, fasting and praying, "Lead us not into temptation," can open the door for God to break your habit of sin. If your heart is hungry for more of Him, He will answer your prayer.

12

Seventh Petition: Deliver Us from the Evil One

I once conducted a seminar for pastors in Hollywood, California, at the local Holiday Inn. As we came to the end of our day together, I asked each pastor to recommit himself to ministry and to the growth of his church. I gave this invitation: "I want you to kneel by your chair, or stand and lift both hands to heaven, or come forward to kneel at the front of the auditorium." Some came to the front of the room to pray, and I walked over to the front row and knelt at an end chair to lead in prayer. I was paraphrasing the Lord's Prayer, and when I came to the seventh petition I said, "Deliver us from the Evil One who would harm us in a traffic accident on the way home. Deliver us from the Evil One who would destroy our health by disease or germs. Deliver us from the Evil One who would hurt us in any way we don't even know about."

I concluded my prayer and then stood to return to the front of the auditorium. Before I made it to the platform, an entire window, including the frame and heavy leaded glass, came crashing down on the chair I had just vacated. Glass scattered in every direction and the sound scared everyone in the room. The audience yelled! Two or three pastors ran to look through the opening to see if anyone was injured on the ground outside. Thankfully, no one was hurt.

Several said they believed God heard my prayer for protection. I don't think the heavy Spanish-style window would have killed me had I still be kneeling at that chair, but then again, you never know. I can't say what *could* have happened, but God's providence was evident to me in what *did* happen. The crash occurred just seconds after I moved away, and I suffered not even a scratch. Did God protect me because I had prayed for deliverance from the Evil One? Was Satan trying to destroy me or destroy the spiritual impact the seminar had made on the pastors? It is entirely possible, because Scripture tells us Satan is trying to destroy every Christian and his or her witness to God's saving power. "Stay alert! Watch out for your great enemy, the devil. He prowls around like a roaring lion, looking for someone to devour" (1 Pet. 5:8, *NLT*).

We've all heard the old adage "An apple a day keeps the doctor away." That's motivation to eat healthy. In Sunday school it was, "A Bible verse a day keeps the Devil away." There may be some truth in that, but the bottom line is, without the power of God, knowing a few Bible verses won't be enough to protect us from the dangers planned for us by Satan.

The seventh petition of the Lord's Prayer is about waging spiritual warfare—and being triumphant. When you pray, "Deliver us from the Evil One," you are confessing that there is, indeed, an Evil One in conflict with God and with you, and that God is your Deliverer from the Devil's schemes. It is a prayer for deliverance.

In the Lord's Army

When you pick up the cross and start following Jesus (see Luke 9:23, *NLT*), you enroll in God's army, with Christ as your commanding officer. The first thing a new recruit does after joining the army is to go to boot camp, where she learns how to follow orders, how to care for herself and other soldiers, how to fight and how to win. We can look at the Lord's Prayer as a spiritual boot camp that trains us to become effective warriors under Christ's command.

The first three petitions focus on our Leader and how to follow His orders. "Hallowed be Thy name" brings you into God's presence and makes you available to His command. "Thy kingdom come" declares your allegiance to God's reign and rule. And "Thy will be done" announces your intention to obey God's will in all things.

The middle petition focuses on what you need for life and ministry. We might think of these needs as supplies for war. "Give us this day our daily bread" is your requisition request to the Commander for what you need to care for yourself and others and to fight the Enemy effectively.

The final three petitions focus on combating the foe. "Forgive us our debts" guards against enemy infiltration and keeps communication lines open between you and the Commander. "Lead us not into temptation" puts you on the alert for potential attacks. And "Deliver us from the Evil One" is your call for supernatural firepower to repel the Enemy. It is a call for reinforcements to protect you and turn the tide of battle to victory.

Life is a test, but it is more than that: It is a war between two powerful (though not equal) armies. The outcome of the war has already been decided (see Rev. 20:7-10), but lesser battles will be waged until the end of time. Satan hates God and you belong to God. Therefore, you will be attacked and must learn to defend yourself.

The Adversary

Paul wrote to the church in Corinth, "When I forgive whatever needs to be forgiven, I do so with Christ's authority for your benefit, so that Satan will not outsmart us. For we are familiar with his evil schemes" (2 Cor. 2:10-11, *NLT*). Are you familiar with Satan's schemes? Do you know who he is and how he operates?

There are fairytales aplenty about the Devil, and too many in our culture—including Christians—have taken these myths as the truth. If you were to ask a dozen people who Satan is and how he works in the world, you would likely get 12 different answers.

On one end of the spectrum, you have folks who imagine the Devil with horns, cloven hooves and a tail, brandishing a pitchfork. This was a popular way to depict Satan in the art of the Middle Ages, but it has no basis in fact. In film and television (the "art" of our modern world), portrayals of the Evil One tend to be dark and sinister, perhaps with black eyes, a goatee and a menacing glare. There is often something appealing about him, however, which reflects renewed interest in the occult in our culture. This interest, even among children and young people, in magic and dark forces is far more dangerous than a pitchfork could ever be.

At the other extreme are folks who deny the existence of Satan altogether. They claim that Satan is not a real entity but only a personification of the evil in the world. The source of evil is not a demonic force opposed to God, but a lack of education, money, hope or diversity. There is no supernatural war being waged just beyond our reality; when the Bible speaks of spiritual warfare, it's just a metaphor. Of course, if Satan is real, the unwillingness to believe it is a gift to him. If no one believes in him, no one will pray against his schemes! In the book of Revelation, the apostle John describes Satan's deceitful nature: "The great dragon, that old serpent, called the Devil, and Satan, which deceiveth the whole world" (Rev. 12:9, *KJV*). If a lack of belief in his existence is any indication, Satan has done an outstanding job of deceiving the whole world. Jesus rightly called the Devil "a murderer . . . a liar and the father of lies" (John 8:44, *NLT*).

Somewhere in the middle are believers who know Satan is real but feel helpless against his schemes and attacks. Nothing could be further from the truth.

During the Civil War, international chess master Paul Morphy visited a chess club in Richmond, Virginia, where on the wall hung an interesting painting.[1] In the picture, Satan plays chess for the soul of a young man, who has found himself in check with only a few of his pieces left to defend himself. It is obvious from the expressions on both their faces that the young man will be defeated and forfeit his soul.

Throughout dinner with the club members, Morphy's eye was continually drawn to the painting. After dinner, he stood before the picture for a few minutes and then declared to the room, "I think that I can take the young man's game and win."[2] No one believed him. All the members of the club had studied the Devil's chessboard and agreed there were no moves the young man could make that would lead to victory. But Morphy insisted, and so the club members set up a chessboard just as the board was set in the painting. Every member took his turn as the Devil, across the table from Morphy, who was playing the young man's pieces. The chess master played one member after another, each time resetting the board to the young man's desperate position.

He won each and every time.

Too many Christians believe they are powerless against the Devil; because of fear and lack of faith, they have surrendered the battle. Still others have been so terrorized by the Evil One's attacks that they are in bondage; they don't know how to fight back. They have forgotten that the Bible declares, "Greater is he that is in you, than he that is in the world" (1 John 4:4, *KJV*).

Satan's name means "adversary." It's an accurate title, because he is opposed to everything God is for. And God is for you (see Rom. 8:31)! The Enemy and his forces of darkness will do all they can to come between you and God's answers to your prayers. He will fight tooth and nail to derail your pursuit of God's will.

That is why you pray, "Deliver us from evil."

The Principles of Victory

Thankfully, God's Word provides a battle plan for every Christian. Sadly, too many believers do not live by the principles of God's Word, and as a result, they don't protect themselves from the attacks of the Evil One. But when you follow God's principles, you not only escape temptation, but you also overcome it—and ultimately win victory over the Enemy.

The Principle of Respect[3]

Yes, Jesus is greater than Satan, but we must have respect for the evil Satan can do to us and to others. If you encounter a fat, three-foot rattlesnake whose mouth is dripping with venom, you respect the snake for the harm it can do to you. You could get bitten if you get playful or overconfident, or if you do not give the snake your full attention.

This does not mean you fear the Devil, just as a trained snake handler does not fear a rattlesnake. But a snake handler does respect the danger posed by the snake. Even though he knows how to handle a snake and how to avoid being bitten, he proceeds with caution. Likewise, you should not fear the Evil One. Fear only God. But respect the potential harm of the Evil One's craftiness and guile. Proceed with caution.

The Principle of Removal

Take an honest look at your life, evaluate your weaknesses and avoid those areas where you are most likely to be tempted. Paul tells us, "Abstain from all appearance of evil" (1 Thess. 5:22, *KJV*). He also says, "Flee these [evil] things" (1 Tim. 6:11, *KJV*).

Do not attempt to attack or even enter into conflict with the Evil One. Look how Scripture prescribes caution in dealings with the Devil: "But even Michael, one of the mightiest of the angels, did not dare accuse the Devil of blasphemy, but simply said, 'The Lord rebuke you!' (This took place when Michael was arguing with the Devil about Moses' body)" (Jude 9, *NLT*).

I once heard the story of a father coming home from work who met his young son in the front yard. "Daddy!" the boy said. "There was a snake in the yard today and I beat him!"

"That's wonderful, Son," Daddy replied. "How did you beat him? With a stick? A rock?"

The boy shook his head. "I beat him running."

As Paul told Timothy, "Run!" (2 Tim. 2:22, *NLT*).

There are some people of God who specialize in spiritual warfare. They have trained and learned from experience how to come against Satan. They know the Word of God and how to confront and cast out demons. God often does the miraculous through people with these gifts, but the average child of God should not directly battle Satan without extensive training and wisdom. Rather, pray daily, "Deliver us from the Evil One," and avoid walking into temptation where you would invite an attack.

The Principle of Resistance

Obviously, the Christian should be active in yielding himself to God. James tells us, "Submit yourselves therefore to God" (Jas. 4:7, *KJV*). That's a wonderful place to begin. Then the apostle adds, "Resist the Devil and he will flee from you." You can protect yourself from Satan's attacks by being proactive in your pursuit of God.

Don't give in to Satan; the apostle Peter said to "stand firm against him, and be strong in your faith" (1 Pet. 5:9, *NLT*). How can you become strong in your faith? Pray and fast! Read, study and memorize the Word. Follow Jesus' example. He fasted and prayed in the wilderness and then was tempted by Satan. With each new temptation, He answered, "It is written . . ." (see Matt. 4:1-11). Resist the Enemy by pursing Christ.

The Principle of Readiness

Jesus told His disciples, "Watch ye and pray lest ye enter into temptation" (Mark 14:38, *KJV*). Keep watch! Stay alert! The apostle Paul advised, "Put on the whole armor of God that you may be able to stand against the wiles of the devil" (Eph. 6:11, *NKJV*). Get ready! Dress yourself for battle!

Fasting and prayer are two keys ways you prepare yourself to withstand the Devil's attacks. When you fast and pray, "Deliver us from the Evil One," you declare your total dependence on God to protect and defend you. You acknowledge that it is His power, not yours, that will overcome the Enemy. The psalmist offered this promise: "The Lord shall preserve you from all evil; he shall preserve your soul. The Lord shall preserve your going out and your coming in from this time forth, and even forevermore" (Ps. 121:7-8, *NKJV*). Get ready by drawing close to your Defender.

Fast for Victory

I pray the Lord's Prayer every day before I get out of bed. I pray in a modern paraphrase:

Lord, You are my heavenly Father.
I want Your name to be holy in my life today.

I want Your kingdom to come in my world.
I yield to your control.
Give me the strength of bread for today.
Forgive my sins as I forgive those who sin against me.
Don't let me face temptations that will destroy me.
Protect me from the Evil One.
May Your kingdom rule in my life.
May Your power give me what I need.
May You get the credit and glory for everything. Amen.

After getting dressed and shaved, and then eating breakfast, I come to my desk to have private time with God. Before I read the Scriptures or look over my prayer list for the day, I again pray the Lord's Prayer. Sometimes I get so wrapped up in worship—"You are my heavenly Father; I want Your name to be holy in my life today"—that I find I've spent the whole time on the first petition! But I never walk away from my time with God without also praying the last petition: "Protect me from the Evil One."

The Enemy is real. I don't expect heavy Spanish-style windows to fall on me at any moment, but I do expect that the Adversary will take any chance he can get to oppose my pursuit of God and my work for His kingdom.

Don't walk away from your time in prayer without asking God for His protection over your life—especially when you are fasting! While the discipline of fasting builds spiritual muscles over the long term, it can also leave you weak and vulnerable in the short term. You need God's presence, protection and deliverance more than ever. "Deliver us from the Evil One" may just save your life, whether from a random drunk driver, the virus going around at work or a demonic-influenced depression.

Rejoice that Satan has no choice but to lose his war with God! And now, fast and pray to win the battles Satan will bring to your doorstep. God will deliver the victory.

Notes

1. "Anecdote of Morphy," *Columbia Chess Chronicle*, Volume 2, Issue 1—Volume 4, Issue 26, 1888, p. 60. Google e-book, http://books.google.com/books?id=Fv42AAAAYAAJ&vq (accessed June 2013).
2. Ibid.
3. These principles first appeared in Elmer Towns, *Theology for Today* (Belmont, CA: Wadsworth Publishing Company, 2nd edition, 2001), pp. 384-385.

Daily Readings for 21 Days of Fasting

Bill Bright, founder of Campus Crusade for Christ, wrote:

> I believe the power of fasting as it relates to prayer is the spiritual atomic bomb that our Lord has given us to destroy the strongholds of evil and usher in a great revival and spiritual harvest around the world. . . . join me in fasting and prayer again and again until we truly experience revival in our homes, our churches, our beloved nation, and throughout the world.[1]

This book is a similar invitation. Now that you know how to fast with the Lord's Prayer, it is time to actually do it! Begin with a one-day Yom Kippur fast, if you are new to fasting, and then undertake longer and longer fasts as your spiritual muscles get strong. In this section, you will find 21 daily devotional readings—three for each of the seven petitions of the Lord's Prayer. A 21-day fast may sound to you now like an unattainable goal, but it isn't. Follow the guidelines in Part I and work up to a long fast. If you do not feel ready to withhold all solid food for such an extended time, consider a Daniel fast, wherein you eat only vegetables or withhold something other than food. With the Spirit's sustaining presence, you can do it.

For each day, there is a recommended Scripture reading and a memory verse to keep you in the Word (and to keep the Word in you). There is also space to write specific prayer requests. You can revisit these lists at the end of your fast to see which prayers God has answered and which requests need more prayer.

I hope these readings will encourage and inspire you as you pursue God's presence in prayer and fasting. The coming revival will begin with believers just like you: so hungry for God that you will give up anything to satisfy your soul.

Note

1. Bill Bright, "Seven Basic Steps to Fasting and Prayer," Campus Crusade for Christ online resource. http://www.cru.org/training-and-growth/devotional-life/7-steps-to-fasting/index.htm (accessed July 2013).

Hallowed Be Thy Name

Day 1

Making a Motel Room into a Sanctuary

I began praying around 6:00 am as always, but my prayers seemed to bounce back. I wasn't getting through to God. I even confessed my frustration as sin, but still the ceiling was lead. My prayers were not lifting my spirit to experience God's presence.

The previous day, my flight out of Lynchburg had been cancelled, so I took the next one. That flight had been delayed because of bad weather, so I missed my evening meal with the pastor (my custom before teaching a seminar). Because my new (delayed) flight would arrive after midnight, the pastor had asked if, instead of him picking me up, would I mind catching a shuttle to the motel? I had agreed, and lived to regret it. After claiming my bags, I had waited 45 minutes in the rain because the shuttle driver was making his rounds as the motel's night watchman. By the time I made it to bed, I was wet, irritable . . . and restless.

The next morning, with only four hours of fitful sleep, that motel room did not look to me like a sanctuary. It felt like a prison.

Then I began to pray the Lord's Prayer, which is how I usually begin my devotions. "Hallowed be Thy name," I prayed, and couldn't go any further. Almost instantly, my prayers focused on the Father and instead of my irritations. I began to worship the Father for His holiness and power. Verses tumbled across my mind and I spoke them aloud, such as: "The heavens declare the glory of God; the skies proclaim the work of his hands" (Ps. 19:1). I praised God for the lightning I had seen arcing across the sky the previous night. Then I started thanking God:

"Thank You for protecting me and the plane during the storm."

"Thank You for getting me to my destination, and that my final flight was not cancelled."

"Thank You for quiet time in the airport to write."

"Thank You for a clean, comfortable bed, and that I didn't have to sleep in an airport."

"Thank You for a hot shower to wake me up."

"Thank You for the opportunity to preach today."

Gradually, I felt the presence of God invade the room. My worship had turned that motel room into a sanctuary, a place where God lives and works. When I worshiped the Father, He came to receive my worship.

The walls no longer bounced back my prayers. Instead, the walls echoed my heart's song as I sang God's praises. God was in the room. I could feel Him. I call this the "atmospheric presence" of God. Just as you can feel moisture in the air even when it's not raining, I felt the presence of God heavy in the room.

After praying for a long time, it was time to meet the pastor and ride with him to the church. I had prayed right through breakfast. But I didn't need to eat. I felt strengthened by the presence of God.

Technically, it was not a fast: I had not planned to fast, nor did I make a vow to fast. It's just that I put God first and forgot to eat. Now that I think about it, that's a pretty good definition for fasting! The Hebrew word for "fast" is *tason*, which suggests that our eating schedule is interrupted by something more important. Worship had interrupted my breakfast time and my hunger. Eating just wasn't as important as spending time with my heavenly Father.

As you begin your fast, don't focus on food or on other things you have decided to give up. Focus on God. If you worship the Father,

He will come to receive your praise and fellowship. Focus on worship that pleases Him, and believe in faith that you will find Him when you seek (see Matt. 7:7). Fasting with the Lord's Prayer is an act of faith. Remember, "Without faith it is impossible to please God" (Heb. 11:6). He will reward you with His presence.

Date Read: ______________________________

Scripture Reading: Isaiah 6

Memory Verse: "But without faith it is impossible to please Him, for he who comes to God must believe that He is, and that He is a rewarder of those who diligently seek Him" (Heb. 11:6, *NKJV*).

Prayer Requests: ______________________________

____

____

____

____

____

____

____

____

Day 2

Hi, Father

When my wife was a little girl, she knelt each evening with her family for devotions. Once, she listened to her father pray, and then it was her turn. She began, "Hi, Father."

Ruth's mother let her finish praying, but then suggested a more reverential appeal to God. Ruth didn't understand why she was being corrected; she had begun her prayer just the way her father always began his! It was only years later that she realized her father began his prayers by heavily breathing out, "Our Heavenly Father." To her young ears, it sounded like, "Hi, Father."

Ruth's brother David was always mischievous, and for a long time he began his prayers, "Hi, God! It's a beautiful day down here. How's it up there with You?"

David's mother and father put a stop to it, more because he was insincere than anything. If he had been sincere, that might have been a fine way to begin a prayer. After all, God wants us to come to Him just as we are. God gladly accepts the prayers of young children and new Christians who haven't learned the "proper" terms—as long as they are seeking Him with a sincere heart.

But as Christians mature and get to know the Scriptures, they learn how God's people approach Him in prayer and the designations they should use. There is no single name to use when addressing God; there are many used in Scripture. When you're not sure how to call on God, I'd advise you to use one of the Bible's names for God. Who first thought up the name

Elohim, or Adonai, or Yahweh, or Jesus? Not me. Not you. Not anyone. God has revealed His names to tell us who He is and what He does. We learn His nature from His names.

Because of my wife's early experiences, I've been a student of the names by which people call on God when they begin to pray.

My pastor at the First Baptist Church in Dallas, Texas, Dr. W. A. Criswell, would usually begin, "Master . . ." then pause silently. It was an invitation to meditate on my servant relationship to God.

Some begin, "God," which emphasizes God's role as Creator and my role as one of His creations.

Some begin, "Lord," reminding me that He owns everything and has the power to answer my prayers.

Some begin, "King," highlighting God's vast power and reminding me that He is my ruler; I am coming to Him for royal favors.

Some begin, "Jesus," pointing me to the Man of Galilee who performed miracles and rose from the dead. Therefore, He can do miracles for me.

Some begin, "Lamb of God," recalling that He is the One who shed His blood to save me from sin and death.

I like to begin, "Our Father who art in heaven." It reminds me that I have an intimate family relationship to God. He is my heavenly Father, who cares for me and listens to my prayer.

The name by which you call on God reveals your attitude toward Him. What do you call Him?

Date Read: ______________________

Scripture Reading: John 14

Memory Verse: "You can ask for anything in my name, and I will do it, so that the Son can bring glory to the Father. Yes, ask me for anything in my name, and I will do it!" (John 14:13-14, *NLT*).

Prayer Requests: ______________________

Day 3

Fathers Want Their Children to Be Happy

My daddy was a heavy-drinking man. If he got to the bar on payday before he got home, there was often not enough money left for food, rent and family needs. So at noon every Saturday, my mother waited at the cash register of White's Hardware Store. She knew if she didn't get some money when Daddy was paid, bills wouldn't get paid and groceries wouldn't be bought.

When the clock struck 12 and the store closed for the day, the owner of White's, Jack White, would come out of his office and wait until the last customer was gone. Then he would open my daddy's cash drawer and count out $52. He'd point to a receipt and say, "Sign it."

There was no Social Security or income tax withholding; money just passed from owner to worker. Daddy would sign, and then Jack White and all the other clerks would make themselves scarce. They knew fireworks were about to explode.

"I need $32," Mother demanded, getting into Daddy's face.

"Erin, don't embarrass me," he yelled.

"If I don't get it now, you'll drink it up."

Back and forth they argued, every Saturday. Mother had a fist full of bills that needed to be paid, and when she finally got her money, she walked from one place to the next to pay them, ending up at the grocery store to get the week's supply.

Like Jack White and the other clerks, I waited until the fireworks were over. Then I spoke up, "Can I have a quarter to go to the movies?"

"Sure you can." Daddy smiled and dug deep in a pocket full of change to find 25 cents, holding it at arm's length to make sure it was a quarter. "Here you go . . . have a great time."

My father loved movies and he loved me. He always fussed with Mother about paying the bills, but he loved to give me a quarter for the Saturday afternoon cowboy matinee.

My wife once asked me if I ever asked for less than a quarter because there was financial pressure. "No," I told her, "I always asked for 25 cents."

"Why?"

"Because I knew my father wanted me to have it. My father loved me."

Your heavenly Father loves you and wants to give you His best. He allows you to make money to use for His glory. He gives you opportunities to serve Him. He sometimes allows problems to test you and make you strong. He also sometimes says no because He wants to protect you.

Today, thank your heavenly Father for the good things He's given you—not just money and material blessings, but *all* the good things such as health, family, a sound mind and freedom to worship Him. Life offers us plenty of strife—I think now of Mother and Daddy arguing over money—because strife is inevitable in an imperfect world peopled by sinful human beings. In the midst of strife, our Father offers us good gifts because He loves us.

As I look back, a quarter for the Saturday cowboy matinee seems childish. But I was a child, and the movies seemed big and important at the time. I thank my heavenly Father for giving me an earthly father who loved me and wanted me to have fun at the movies.

You probably have concerns that seem big and important to you now. Perhaps your concerns are "childish" to our heavenly Father, but He doesn't put us down because we act like children. We are *His* children, and He loves us. He wants our lives to be abundant (see John 10:10). Whatever problems or strife you are facing, step away and wait on your heavenly Father. He has a "quarter" for you today. You need only to ask.

Date Read: ______________________________

Scripture Reading: Psalm 37

Memory Verse: "Delight yourself also in the Lord, and He shall give you the desires of your heart" (Ps. 37:4, *NKJV*).

Prayer Requests: ______________________________

Thy Kingdom Come

Day 4

There's Always Room for One More

I grew up in Savannah, Georgia, in the neighborhood of Wagner Heights, where there were eight other boys around my age. We called ourselves the Cuckoo Patrol, and we played together constantly. Most of the time we played in my yard because my mother loved little boys and pretty well let us do what we wanted (which was to have as much fun as possible every waking minute).

Our yard was cluttered, not at all like the neighbors' nicely manicured lawns. The big tree held aloft an always-expanding tree house (built by boys) and a rope swing that could launch us from the porch to the middle of the yard. Mother let me build a pigeon pen in addition to the chicken coop, and the bird noises and smells added to the disarray. On top of all that, Mother let us dig foxholes so we could fight World War II, which was going on in Europe and the Pacific, with our homemade guns right in the front yard.

At the end of a long day in the trenches, Mother would call, "Y'all wanna come in and watch Elmer eat?"

My buddies knew that was their invitation to the table, which had an eight-foot bench on one side and four chairs on the other. Mother loved to feed boys and they loved to eat her food. She had grown up a farm girl, and there is nothing like farm cooking. She never threw away leftovers but always had several covered dishes in the fridge that she could quickly warm up. We might or might not have meat, but there were always lots of veggies. By the time she had everything warmed up, the table usually looked like a Thanksgiving meal. Don't even think about matched plates, but hungry boys don't care about fancy dinnerware. We'd use bread to sop up juice or bits of food left on any plate or bowl—including the serving dishes.

"There's always room for one more," she'd say when a late buddy showed up at the kitchen door. We could always squeeze another body on that eight-foot bench.

To me, that is a picture of God's table. *There's always room for one more.* "The Lord . . . is not willing that any should perish, but that all should come to repentance" (2 Pet. 3:9, *NKJV*). There is plenty of room in God's family for any and all.

When you pray for God's kingdom to come on earth, you're asking for God's rule to extend to those who are not yet Christians. You're praying for unsaved people to become Christians and join us at God's table. God wants to answer this prayer more than anything because *there's always room for one more*. Why does God make more room at His table? Because, like my mother, He loves people and loves to feed them.

God has a refrigerator filled with lots of good things to eat. The food is not only good tasting, but it is also good for you. When you eat the Bread of Life, you will grow and become strong—and there's always more if you're still hungry. You don't have to sop the serving dishes, because God has more food for you than you can possibly eat. I've been eating God's food for 63 years and I've never exhausted its supply. And if I go away hungry, it's my own fault.

Pray, "Thy kingdom come," into the life of family and friends who are not saved. Yes, you don't want them to go to hell; that's proper motivation to pray. And yes, you don't want them to continue hurting themselves with sinful, selfish lives. But even more: Remember the good and soul-filling times you've had at God's table. Pray that God's kingdom would come into their lives because you want them to enjoy the same good things and be satisfied.

Date Read: ______________________________

Scripture Reading: John 6:1-40

Memory Verse: "And Jesus said to them, 'I am the bread of life. He who comes to Me shall never hunger, and he who believes in Me shall never thirst'" (John 6:35, *NKJV*).

Prayer Requests: ______________________________

Day 5

Preaching the Gospel to Every Person in the World

In the spring of 1973, Jerry Falwell called for Thomas Road Baptist Church and Liberty University to fast for world evangelism. But his challenge was not just theoretical. He had a plan to present the gospel to every people group in the world on one Sunday.

Dr. Falwell preached weekly on the *Old Time Gospel Hour*, broadcast on 210 television stations and hundreds of radio stations across the nation, covering 95 percent of the U.S. population. But he had a vision for a much wider reach: "Let's preach the gospel over every missionary radio station in the world." Then he added, "And let's do it on the same day."

He invited the church, the university and any other believers to fast and pray on and leading up to the appointed day. Besides obeying Jesus' command to preach the gospel in every nation, Dr. Falwell had an additional motivation. "We will hasten the return of Jesus Christ by preaching to everyone in the world." And he quoted from the Gospel of Matthew: "And this gospel of the kingdom shall be preached in all the world for a witness unto all nations, and then shall the end come" (Matt. 24:14, *KJV*).

I couldn't think of a better way to pray, "Thy kingdom come." We could preach the gospel worldwide! When the last person to hear the gospel was saved, Jesus would return for His church.

We found out that, technically, we couldn't do it all on one day. Missionary radio stations didn't broadcast in every language every day; they used the same channel to broadcast in different languages on different days of the week. So we adjusted our expectations to include a week instead of one day! There were many details to be ironed out before the target week. We had to raise money to purchase time on various radio and TV stations. We had to hire hundreds of translators to preach in hundreds of languages, and to make sure they did it with passion and clarity. We had to raise money to pay them.

Jesus had challenged His disciples, "Go into all the world and preach the gospel to every creature" (Mark 16:15, *NKJV*). We were going into all the world on radio and television. We were presenting the gospel in the languages of the people of the world. Much of the Communist world was closed to missionaries at that time, but we crossed closed borders on the airwaves.

I came to that fast with great anticipation. We were serious about the Great Commission, and we were making an honest attempt to do it in a single week. As I fasted, I interceded for the gospel invitation at the end of the sermon: "Lord, save souls." I fasted with great eagerness. While I couldn't go to every nation of the world, I could go there by intercession. While I couldn't preach the gospel in every language, I could pray in my own language and God would hear me. Then God could work through each sermon to win to Christ some from every tribe, every language and every nation.

When you pray, "Thy kingdom come," you are praying for the effectiveness of gospel preaching around the world. You are asking for the kingdom of Jesus Christ to rule in hearts across the globe. You are praying for His reign to redeem and restore every culture.

When you pray, "Thy kingdom come," you are praying for individuals to be saved. You are praying over the unsaved among your family, friends, coworkers and acquaintances. You are asking God to save them and to rule in their lives.

I remember that spring day in 1973, fasting and praying for the effectiveness of gospel preaching around the world. I remember the enthusiasm of my prayer. That's the kind of passion we should each bring to our prayer, "Thy kingdom come."

Date Read: ________________________________

Scripture Reading: Mark 16:1-20

Memory Verse: "Go into all the world and preach the gospel to every creature" (Mark 16:15, *NKJV*).

Prayer Requests: ________________________________

____
____
____
____
____
____
____
____
____
____

Day 6

The King Must Rule His Kingdom

When I was a boy growing up in Wagner Heights, Harry Conley was the leader of our little gang, the Cuckoo Patrol. Among the nine of us, he was the natural leader and he always decided what we would do, whether digging foxholes, exploring the three cemeteries next door or playing tackle football in a plowed field. We always enjoyed doing whatever Harry decided, because he was a good leader.

But a day came when we democratically elected a new leader for the Cuckoo Patrol. Perhaps we had tired of Harry's leadership, or others of us wanted a chance to lead. I don't really remember. Three boys were nominated, including me. I won the election and became president of the Cuckoo Patrol.

"Let's play tackle football," I said around noon one Saturday, heading into the house to get my football.

"No," Harry vetoed the idea. "Let's all go to the movie theater downtown."

All the guys agreed with this plan, following Harry down the road.

Running after them, I objected, "But, guys, I'm the president."

It didn't make any difference who had the title, because Harry was the leader. There are too many people who claim Jesus as the Lord of their life but act like the Cuckoo Patrol. They elect Jesus as their president but then follow Harry Conley, their old nature. They may claim to follow Jesus, but they do whatever their old nature wants to do.

When you pray, "Thy kingdom come," you're asking for the rule of God to guide your life. To understand what this means, let's look at the characteristics of a kingdom. First, every kingdom needs a king who leads and makes decisions for and about those under his rule. Is Jesus your King? Does Christ make the decisions by which you run your life?

Second, every kingdom has laws by which the citizens live. When you become a citizen of the Kingdom of heaven, you agree to abide by the Ten Commandments: no stealing, no lying, no murder, no adultery, no coveting. The most important of the Commandments is to love and honor God above all else and to love your neighbor as yourself (see Matt. 22:37-40).

Third, every kingdom needs a purpose, a unifying vision. Jesus said, "If any of you wants to be my follower, you must turn from your selfish ways, take up your cross daily, and follow me" (Luke 9:23, *NLT*). Because Jesus is our King, we must live for Him and put Him first in all that we do. We live by the laws of the King and we live to please the King. "Seek the Kingdom of God above all else, and live righteously, and he will give you everything you need" (Matt. 6:33, *NLT*).

Fourth, a kingdom offers privileges to its citizens. If Jesus is your King, you have the privilege of calling on Him at any time. He will answer your prayers. When you get into trouble, He will come to help you. "In my desperation I prayed, and the Lord listened; he saved me from all my troubles" (Ps. 34:6, *NLT*). You also have the privilege of the King's presence. While most kings sit on the throne, far removed from the average citizen, Jesus said, "I am with you always, even to the end of the age" (Matt. 28:20, *NLT*).

Fifth, a kingdom offers its citizens protection. No matter where you go, your citizenship in God's kingdom affords you the protection of the King. He will defend you from attack. "The Lord keeps you from all harm and watches over your life. The Lord keeps watch over you as you come and go, both now and forever" (Ps. 121:7-8, *NLT*).

Today when you pray, "Thy kingdom come," pray that it will come in your life in a real and powerful way. You are a citizen of heaven—starting living like it!

Date Read: ______________________________

Scripture Reading: Psalm 2:1-12

Memory Verse: "Where is He who has been born King of the Jews? For we have seen His star in the East and have come to worship Him" (Matt. 2:2, *NKJV*).

Prayer Requests:______________________________

____

____

____

____

____

____

____

____

____

Thy Will Be Done

Day 7

Sure, Why Not?

When I got to college, I tried to date all the pretty girls. But they all had excuses like, "I've got to wash my hair" or "I've got a term paper to write." Really, they were all saying, "No." There was probably a reason. I was young (17), had acne and looked like a high school freshman, not a college freshman.

An older student got me started writing a prayer journal, and instead of playing the field, I decided to pray for the very best for me, a girl who would be God's will for me. So I wrote down that she had to be interested in godly things and faithful in her studies. She needed to be a diligent worker and modest in her dress. And I added that her father should have money because I was poor.

Ruth Forbes fit the description, so I banged on the window of heaven and asked God, "Make her say yes when I ask for a date!" I caught Ruth in the hallway and suggested we go out together on Friday evening.

She responded, "Sure, why not?"

I went back to my dorm room and wrote a great big AMEN! next to that prayer request. (I still have that page from my journal.)

Ten months later, I was ready to ask Ruth to be my wife, so I banged on heaven's window again and asked God to make me the happiest man in the world. I got a red rose, wrote my proposal in a poem and got on my knees to ask the woman I loved to make the biggest decision of our life together. "Ruth, will you marry me?"

"Sure, why not!"

(She actually said, "Yes." But the way I tell it makes a better story.)

Do you cover every major decision in prayer? When you pray, "Thy will be done," you are asking God to guide every decision. He has a plan for you that involves every area of life, including your mate. If you are not yet married, pray that He will guide you to connect with the right person. If you are already married, pray that He will strengthen you to be faithful and loving to your spouse.

Pray about your life's work, including how to prepare for your vocation (such as college or apprenticeship) and what jobs to accept or refuse. Pray that the right doors would open to give you opportunities to serve God in your career.

Pray about major purchases such as a house, car, appliances, and so on. Because your monthly payments impact your life, make sure you can glorify God in what you possess and how you handle your money.

Pray about joining the armed services, changing jobs and moving to another city. Pray about making decisions that affect your children, such as where to send them to school and what extra-curricular activities to allow. Pray over your daily schedule and your checkbook, both of which are hinge points in your life with God.

There are many ways to apply the prayer, "Thy will be done." First, *yield your daily schedule to God*. Obviously God will not tell you audibly what to do each day. You will plan your day with His priorities in mind, asking what is best for your family, your health, your job, your growth, and so on. Then, throughout the day, look for His guidance in the situations you are praying about. When you say, "Sure, why not?" to God's values and direction, you will do His will in your daily life.

Second, *ask for God's providential guidance*. Providence is when God works behind the scenes to "work all things according to His will" (Rom. 8:28). Providence is when God acts like the director of a play. He sets the stage and guides you as you prepare, but you are the actor who says the lines, acts out the scene and uses the props He has given you to use. When you say, "Sure, why not?" to God's providence, He will guide you to do His will in the grand story He is writing for you.

Third, *ask for God's protection.* When you yield to God's plan for your life and attempt to walk in His will, expect Him to protect you. The Bible does not promise that life will always be a rose garden; persecution, trials and temptations are to be expected. But when you say, "Sure, why not?" to God's plan, He will protect you so that you can complete it.

Even if you pray, "Thy will be done," and God leads you into the valley of the shadow of death, rejoice. He will lead you *through* the valley. He will not leave you there. He will meet you on the other side.

Date Read: ________________________________

Scripture Reading: Psalm 23

Memory Verse: "And we know that all things work together for good to those who love God, to those who are the called according to His purpose" (Rom. 8:28, *NKJV*).

Prayer Requests: ____________________________

Day 8

Don't Ever Have Your First Cigarette

Eastern Heights Presbyterian Church never had more than 60 or 70 people and never accomplished much as a congregation. But it had one Sunday school teacher who impacted my life. One beautiful, sunny morning between Sunday school and the worship service, all the men had gone outside to smoke cigarettes. (In those days, it was more common to smoke than not to, even among churchgoing folks.) I was about 10 years old and stood outside with my teacher, Jimmy Breland, and three or four other boys.

"Don't ever have your first cigarette," Jimmy said, pointing to a man tapping out a Lucky Strike on his pack, ready to light up.

"Why, Jimmy?" I asked.

"You'll burn up a bunch of money." Jimmy explained that a pack of cigarettes cost about 20 cents each, which meant that smokers burned up a penny every time they lit up. He turned to me. "Do you like to burn up money, Elmer?" I think he asked because he knew my mother and father smoked, plus all six of my uncles on my father's side and seven uncles on my mother's side.

"No, sir," I chirped.

"When you smoke, it's like burning up a dollar bill." Jimmy reached down and swooped his hand over the grass. "It's like rolling your own cigarette in a dollar bill and then burning it up." Then he said again, "Don't ever smoke your first cigarette."

But he didn't stop with a warning. Our teacher commanded, "Put up your right hand." We all raised our right hand like someone being sworn into the service or onto a witness stand. Then he had us repeat after him: "I promise . . . never to smoke . . . my first cigarette . . . so help me God."

Although everyone in my family smoked, I never have smoked my first cigarette. I look back on that day and thank God for Jimmy Breland. And I marvel at the power of the will that keeps even a little guy like I was from giving into the pressure to do what everyone else is doing.

When you pray, "Thy will be done," you are doing what I did that sunny Sunday morning when I was 10 years old. You are holding up your hand and pledging to obey Jesus Christ in everything.

Yes, you will struggle with the inclinations and desires of your old nature. Even the great apostle Paul did: "I want to do what is good, but I don't. I don't want to do what is wrong, but I do it anyway" (Rom. 7:19, *NLT*). But you can cultivate a habit of obedience by praying each day, "Thy will be done." Start an obedience habit instead of a cigarette habit.

Establish a rule for your life like young Elmer Towns did so long ago. Make a commitment, so help you God, to do God's will, not your own or anyone else's. Then, when you pray, "Thy will be done" each day, surrender your life anew to His purpose and plan.

Date Read: ____________________________

Scripture Reading: Romans 12

Memory Verse: "I beseech you therefore, brethren, by the mercies of God, that you present your bodies a living sacrifice, holy, acceptable to God, which is your reasonable service" (Rom. 12:1, *NKJV*).

Prayer Requests: ____________________________

Day 9

What Does a Baptist Know About Fasting?

In 1995 I presented the editorial staff of Regal Books, the publisher of this book, with a list of topics on which I felt I would like to write and publish. In the middle of the list appeared "Fasting." I told them no one had done a significant book on fasting in 100 years. They were excited at the prospect of putting out a book on fasting, and discussed two or three of their regular authors who could, perhaps, write on the topic. But everyone on their list was busy with other projects.

I sheepishly raised my hand and said, "I can write the book."

They laughed. "What does a Baptist know about fasting?"

I explained that I had fasted dozens of times at Liberty University, and each year I lectured to the student leadership on fasting. Hearing about my practical experience with the topic, the Regal staff agreed that I should write the book.

I came home and wrestled with ideas, but nothing came. I mentioned my struggles to my wife and Ruth suggested, "Since it's a book on fasting, you ought to fast about writing it."

Genius. Why didn't I think of that?

I spent a one-day Yom Kippur fast praying for God to give me an outline for the book. I scratched out several ideas, but nothing came together. That night I broke my one-day fast and took Ruth out to dinner. She asked, "What did God tell you about the book?"

"Nothing. All I have is a nine-point sermon on fasting . . ."

My words were left hanging in the air, along with my gesturing hands. In my mind's eye, I saw nine chapters, each one addressing a practical accomplishment of fasting, based on the sermon material I already had. The book's overall theme would be that fasting and prayer are practical solutions to real, everyday problems. After all, I had demonstrated that fasting could solve the problem of what to write in a book about fasting. Isn't God good?

As I wrote each of the nine chapters, I fasted once a week about that chapter, asking God to help me write helpful material. I broke each week's fast by taking my wife out to dinner, when I would read the introduction to her and explain its contents. On one such evening she said, "The chapter titles sound academic, like a term paper." If this book was to attract the average Christian, she suggested, it needed chapter titles that would appeal to a popular audience. I tried to defend my titles, but she answered, "Why don't you fast about it?"

I did, and wrote down several suggestions. When I read them to her that evening, Ruth said the new titles were still too academic. We finally dropped the subject and talked about other things. At one point, she mentioned that we needed to send Paula 20 dollars to support her on our church's choir trip. Then Ruth mentioned that the choir was following a Daniel fast to raise money for the trip.

"Stop!" I exclaimed. "That's it!" Suddenly I knew that each of my nine practical points corresponded to a person from the Bible who fasted to solve a practical problem. I grabbed a napkin and wrote down the biblical characters' names next to a list of my chapter topics. That book became *Fasting for Spiritual Breakthrough*, and by God's grace it has touched thousands of people's lives. I fasted and prayed, and God led the way.

When you fast to solve a particular problem, you are really fasting to find God's will. When you pray, "Thy will be done," you are asking God to lead the way through the twists and turns of your life. You are bringing God into your decision-making—or, better, you are bringing your decision-making into your relationship with Him. He's better than a personal coach. He is your heavenly Father, and He will show you His will when you seek Him in fasting and prayer.

Date Read: ____________________

Scripture Reading: Philippians 4:1-23

Memory Verse: "I can do all things through Christ who strengthens me" (Phil. 4:13, *NKJV*).

Prayer Requests: ____________________

Give Us This Day Our Daily Bread

Day 10

A Squirt of Gas for a Burst of Power

An elderly German neighbor in Wagner Heights had an old 1934 Packard in his backyard, and he let the Cuckoo Patrol use our mechanical skills to try to get it running. It was a rusty old frame without a body—just an engine, a steering wheel and tires. It did have two broad front fenders. We experimented on the engine and eventually got it to roar into life. Within seconds, however, it shut down. We squirted gasoline into the fuel pump and it roared again, but only briefly. After many "roars" we discovered there was no fuel tank.

But we decided to drive it anyway.

The youngest boy got behind the wheel while two other guys propped themselves on each front fender, each of them holding a glass of gasoline and a nose dropper. The two took turns squirting gas into the open fuel pump, and how that Packard roared! And then she hiccupped. So they would squirt more gas into the fuel pump, and she would roar again. Then hiccup again.

When you're a young experimentalist, you go with whatcha got.

The youngest boy put the gear into reverse and backed that Packard into Henrietta Street, roaring and hiccupping all the way. The rest of us jumped up and down, yelling and screaming in triumph. Between the roaring hiccup of the Packard and our cheering racket, ladies up and down the block came running to their front doors to see the commotion.

Now came the real test. The driver slipped her into first gear . . . let off the clutch . . . and the old Packard lurched forward! The boys on the front fenders kept squirting drops of gas into the fuel pump, and the car, in fits and starts, roared and hiccupped right on down the street.

We only made it a couple of blocks. The old German man came running out of his house, waving his arms and yelling, "If the engine gets hot and you spill gasoline on it, you'll blow yourselves up!" We had thought our nose-dropper plan was ingenious but, actually, it was suicidal.

Without a fuel tank to supply a steady stream of gas to the fuel pump, that Packard couldn't be what it was made to be. We caught only glimpses, in her occasional roars and forward lurches, of what she might have been with a consistent and reliable supply of fuel.

The phrase "fits and starts" is an accurate description of the way many Christians follow Christ. We hiccup along, occasionally roaring to life and lurching a little farther down the road. Consistency is a big problem, and I believe it's because we don't connect ourselves to a steady stream of fuel. We sit on the fender with a Bible and treat it like a glass of gasoline. We read a verse or two, like a boy squirting gas into a fuel pump with a nose dropper. We roar of Jesus one moment, and the next we fall silent.

Today you prayed, "Give us *this day* our *daily* bread." Have you ever wondered why this petition places such a heavy emphasis on *today*? I believe it reflects our need to connect with God every day. It is only through regular, steady connection with His Spirit that we can follow Christ reliably and consistently. We need to connect ourselves to the Holy Spirit—our full tank of gas—to get daily power to live for God.

Just as gas is the fuel for a 1934 Packard and bread is the fuel for the human body, so too the Holy Spirit is the fuel to energize the child of God. Do you have fuel to run for God today?

Date Read: ______________________________

Scripture Reading: Romans 8:1-17

Memory Verse: "And do not be drunk with wine, in which is dissipation; but be filled with the Spirit" (Eph. 5:18, *NKJV*).

Prayer Requests: ______________________________

Day 11

You'll Shoot Your Eye Out

Sometimes we don't get our prayers answered because we treat God like Santa Claus. A child runs to sit on Santa's lap and then babbles all the things she wants for Christmas, barely taking a breath and never letting Saint Nick get a word in edgewise. But the heavenly Father is not like Santa Claus. Don't begin praying with your "wish list." Begin with worship: "Hallowed be Thy name." Then focus on the expansion of God's rule: "Thy kingdom come." Then surrender your will to God's: "Thy will be done." Only after you have done these are you ready to ask for the things you want.

Many of us know the story of Ralphie, the little boy in *A Christmas Story* who wants a "Red Ryder carbine-action, two hundred shot Range Model air rifle with a compass in the stock and this thing which tells time." And Ralphie does everything he can think of to make sure he gets it. He leaves clues around the house for his father and mother to find, even slipping notices in the magazines they read. A Red Ryder BB gun is his heart's desire.

But every adult, including the local Santa Claus, who hears Ralphie's dearest Christmas wish has only one thing to say: "You'll shoot your eye out!"

Our providential God is in the business of meeting needs. When you pray, "Give us this day our daily bread," you are, first and foremost, praying that God will meet your real, tangible, daily needs such as for food, shelter and a way to pay the bills. Bread is basic and universal—every culture has a version of a simple starch that is a staple of the daily diet. The Lord's Prayer does not say, "Give us this day our cinnamon rolls with extra icing" or "Give us this day our artisan-crafted garlic loaf." The "bread" Jesus tells us to pray for daily is the essential stuff of life. He also reminds us that "your Father knows exactly what you need even before you ask him!" (Matt. 6:8, *NLT*). You can trust your heavenly Father to provide what you need.

But that doesn't mean the Father isn't interested in giving you good gifts that are not strictly necessities. Every good earthly father wants to give his children toys and fun activities just because he loves them and wants them to be happy. Ralphie wants a Red Ryder BB gun—which seems like a necessity to him but, of course, is not. There are many reasons Ralphie's parents might refuse his request, including the very real danger of shooting his eye out. But because they love him, Ralphie gets his gun. Likewise, the heavenly Father loves you and wants to give you good gifts. You may receive what you want, or something even better, or something different that is more satisfying.

Then again, you may not receive what you ask for. God can see that the thing you want will cause you harm now or in the future. He can see what effect it will have on your relationship with Him and with others. He can see that "you'll shoot your eye out."

Ask God to meet your needs, then ask Him for your heart's desire. But then trust Him to know if and when to grant your request. When you pray, "Give us this day our daily bread," you are expressing your confidence in God's ability to provide for your needs and prioritize your wants.

Seek after His heart and His will, and the things you ask for will align with His will for your life. "Take delight in the Lord, and he will give you your heart's desires" (Ps. 37:4).

Date Read: ______________________________

Scripture Reading: Matthew 7:1-12

Memory Verse: "Ask, and it will be given to you; seek, and you will find; knock, and it will be opened to you. For everyone who asks receives, and he who seeks finds, and to him who knocks it will be opened" (Matt. 7:7-8, *NKJV*).

Prayer Requests: ______________________________

____

____

____

____

____

____

____

____

____

____

____

____

____

____

Day 12

Once You Begin, Don't Let Up or Stop

I thought my uncle, Johnny Newsome, was the most important railroad man in the world. He was the switchman in Burroughs, Georgia, the only place between New York and Miami where two great railroads crossed: the Atlantic Coast Line and the Seaboard Railway. He could stop powerful locomotives just by throwing a lever.

One Sunday afternoon Uncle Johnny and I walked about a mile down the tracks to a large warehouse full of potatoes. He discovered that the locomotives had hauled away the loaded boxcar, but hadn't put an empty boxcar in its place for the workers to fill the following day.

"Let's move the boxcar in place," he said. His eyes twinkled like he was up to something.

"You don't have your pole," I pointed out. Uncle Johnny moved heavy boxcars with a six-foot steel pole that had a lever at one end to slide between a wheel and the tracks. With a prying motion, he could move a boxcar that weighed thousands of pounds.

"Let's push it into place."

"It's too heavy!" I protested.

"No," he said. "Every force produces some reaction. If you jumped up and down right now, you'd shake the earth. Only you couldn't see it move because the reaction would be so small."

"Like this?" I jumped up and down a couple of times.

He just laughed.

We walked to the end of the empty boxcar and Uncle Johnny showed me how to position both my feet on a cross tie and my shoulder against the car. "Don't push too hard or you will wear out," he warned. "But once we get the boxcar moving, we have to keep pushing. Once you begin, don't let up or stop."

We started pushing, and talked about other things. Uncle Johnny was quite a talker when his wife, Aunt Pauline, was not around. After about five minutes, I thought my feet were slipping off the cross tie, but Uncle Johnny said the car was moving. It didn't look that way to me, but then I spied a line between the hitch and a rock on the ground. Sure enough, the boxcar was moving away from that line. I couldn't believe it! We were pushing a boxcar with only our brute strength! (I hadn't noticed the boxcar sat on a slight decline that helped with momentum once we got it moving.)

You have been fasting and praying for nearly two weeks. It's usually about this time that some people violate their fast or quit praying toward their prayer goal. Why? For many, it's because they haven't seen an answer or any movement toward an answer. People quit praying for many reasons. Some get discouraged. Some let doubt get to them. Some have formed a habit of quitting. Some let sin overtake them—they say, "Why keep fasting? I've sinned." They might as well eat and enjoy themselves.

Don't quit. God may be moving toward an answer, and if you stop, He'll stop. It's like the boxcar: You can't see what's happening, but God is moving. "Men always ought to pray and not lose heart" (Luke 18:1, *NKJV*). If your request was important enough to make a vow to not eat, keep on praying and keep on fasting until you fulfill your vow.

What will you get if you give up? Only something to eat.

Keep praying and fasting. Don't let up or stop.

Date Read: ____________________________________

Scripture Reading: Luke 18:1-14

Memory Verse: "Men always ought to pray and not lose heart" (Luke 18:1, *NKJV*).

Prayer Requests: ______________________________

Forgive Us Our Debts

Day 13

It Was So Good, I Wanted to Save It

I remember the first bald-faced lie I ever told. I probably told "smaller" ones before that, but the first one I can recall was a doozie.

I began attending Waters Avenue School in Savannah, Georgia, in 1938. Our school was among the first to offer hot lunches to children whose parents worked in the Savannah shipyards. The empty caverns of the basement were converted to a modern cafeteria, with steam tables and bright murals on the walls.

I was in line, watching the cafeteria workers plop various food groups on my plate. I didn't want any slaw because it was just cut-up raw cabbage with no dressing. I said, "I don't want any of that. My mother doesn't serve it at home."

Plop. The worker said, "It's good for you."

At my table, I took a bite and gagged on the dry cabbage. It wouldn't go down, so I spit it out and hid it in a napkin. The same thing happened on the second fork full. I just couldn't eat the stuff.

In those days, there was a guard at the door who wouldn't let us go to recess unless we cleaned our plates. (That was considered a moral attribute back then.) But I figured out a way to outfox the cafeteria police: I filled my pocket and planned to drop the dry slaw on the playground during recess.

Back in class, I felt the cabbage in my pocket. I had forgotten to drop it on the playground. *I'll drop it in the street on the way home.* But I forgot that plan, too. That night as I was getting in bed, Mother was hanging up my pants. She said, "What is this slaw doing in your pocket?"

That's when I told my first big lie: "Mother, it was so good, I wanted to keep it."

We all lie. David wrote, "I said in my haste, 'All men are liars'" (Ps. 116:11, *KJV*). He could have taken all day and come to the same conclusion! But not only men lie; women lie, teens lie and children lie. Along with all kinds of liars, there are all kinds of lies: little lies and big lies, white lies and whoppers, intentional and unintentional, justifying lies. Lies come from our sinful hearts and Scripture teaches that "everyone has sinned" (Rom. 3:23, *NLT*).

Many people think that lying is not really bad. Everyone needs to cover up a mistake once in a while. But there are three really bad things about lying. First, it hurts our character for we know the truth in our hearts. A lie weakens our moral resolve. Second, it hurts others because it violates their trust in us. They may also live wrongly when we mislead them. Third, lying offends God because He is truth. How can we say the Spirit of truth lives within us if we refuse to acknowledge lying as a sin?

What's the result of lying? "But cowards, unbelievers, the corrupt, murderers, the immoral, those who practice witchcraft, idol worshipers, and all liars—their fate is in the fiery lake of burning sulfur. This is the second death" (Rev. 21:8, *NLT*). We lie because we are sinners, and sinners go to hell. But Jesus took our punishment on the cross! He died for every sin, including every lie. Those who have come to Jesus for the forgiveness of sins know "the blood of Jesus Christ His Son cleanses us from all sin" (1 John 1:7, *NKJV*).

When you pray, "Forgive us our debts," each day, you remember Christ's sacrifice that saved you from the wages of sin. But you also ask the Father to forgive the white lies, greed, lust, gossip and other sins that disrupt your relationship with Him and others. His forgiveness tears down the barriers sin puts up and sets your feet on praying ground.

Don't rationalize your sins or blame others. The cafeteria workers were not to blame for my lie. No, only I was responsible for my choice to sin. And only by asking for forgiveness from my heavenly Father and my earthly mother could those relationships be set right.

Date Read: ______________________________

Scripture Reading: Romans 3:10-28

Memory Verse: "If we confess our sins, He is faithful and just to forgive us our sins and to cleanse us from all unrighteousness" (1 John 1:9, *NKJV*).

Prayer Requests:___________________________

____

____

____

____

____

____

____

____

Day 14

Remember the Duck

Young Tommy got a slingshot for his birthday and took it with him when he went to visit his grandmother on the farm. When he arrived, Tommy ran into the backyard, shot at a fencepost and missed. He went into the woods, shot at a flying bird and missed. He walked down to the creek, shot at a snake and missed. Dejected, he returned to the farmyard, shot at Grandmother's favorite duck, hit it between the eyes and killed it.

Tommy looked in every direction and didn't see a soul. Believing no one had seen him, he gathered up the corpse of the duck, found a shovel in the tool shed and buried it behind the barn.

That night after dinner, Grandmother asked Tommy's sister, Mary Ann, to wash the dirty dishes.

"Oh no," Mary Ann said. "Tommy loves to wash dishes. He'll do it." Then she whispered in his ear, "*Remember the duck.*" Tommy washed the dishes.

The next morning, Grandmother asked Mary Ann to sweep the hall and front porch.

"Oh no!" she replied. "Tommy loves to sweep." And she again she hissed, "*Remember the duck.*"

For days, Tommy did all of Mary Ann's chores in addition to his own. He folded clothes, did the sweeping and, of course, washed all the dishes. Each time Mary Ann was called on to do a chore, she whispered, "*Remember the duck.*"

By the end of the week, Tommy couldn't stand it any longer. He found Grandmother and confessed, "I killed your duck." He cried, telling her how sorry he was and how he didn't mean to kill it.

"I know," Grandmother said. "I was at the kitchen window and saw you do it. I saw you panic and try to hide what you'd done." She gave him a comforting hug. "I forgave you when I was looking through the window." Then she added, "My biggest concern was not for my duck; it was for you. Why did you let Mary Ann keep you in bondage?"

There are many Christians in bondage to a past sin. They know on a rational level that God forgives, but they are haunted by guilt. Again and again they hear a hiss, "*Remember the duck.*" But instead of a duck, it's a divorce, or time in prison, or a rage-filled outburst at their kids. Whatever it was, shame keeps them in bondage and keeps them from full, loving fellowship with the heavenly Father.

When you pray, "Forgive us our debts," act on the integrity of the Lord's Prayer and seek God's forgiveness—and accept it. If you sincerely pray, "Forgive my debt," God will do three things. First, He will forgive you. "But if we confess our sins to him, he is faithful and just to forgive us" (1 John 1:9, *NLT*). But it doesn't end there.

"But if we confess our sins to him, he is faithful . . . to cleanse us from all wickedness" (1 John 1:9, *NLT*). After forgiving you, God wipes out the record in heaven of your wickedness. If you feel continuing shame for past sins God has forgiven, your guilty conscience has more authority in your life than God! Your record is clean, now allow the Spirit to clean your conscience as well. Don't listen to the voice of shame: "*Remember the duck.*" God has forgiven and forgotten, and now you can live as a cleansed child of God.

The third thing God does when you pray, "Forgive my debt," is renew His fellowship with you. "We are lying if we say we have fellowship with God but go on living in spiritual darkness; we are not practicing the truth. But if we are living in the light, as God is in the light . . . the blood of Jesus, his Son, cleanses us from all sin" (1 John 1:6-7, *NLT*). You have come out of darkness of sin into the Light of Christ, and you have fellowship with the Father.

Instead of remembering the duck, remember this: "He has removed our sins as far from us as the east is from the west. The Lord is like a father to his children, tender and compassionate to those who fear him" (Ps. 103:11-12, *NLT*).

Date Read: ______________________________

Scripture Reading: Mark 11:22-26

Memory Verse: "And whenever you stand praying, if you have anything against anyone, forgive him, that your Father in heaven may also forgive you your trespasses" (Mark 11:25, *NKJV*).

Prayer Requests:___________________________

____

____

____

____

____

____

Day 15

I'm Busy, Get Somebody Else

My son went to the college where I was a teacher. One day I had to go to the airport to pick up an important person and my schedule was packed, so I asked my son to run my car through the wash and sweep the trash out of the floorboards. I wanted to make a good impression on my important visitor.

"I'm busy, Dad, get somebody else." He listed for me all the things he had to do. To my ears they sounded trivial, especially when compared to the visitor I thought was so impressive.

My son didn't help me with the car, yet somehow I got it clean and picked up my visitor. But I was miffed because I paid for his gas and helped him with his car expenses. Why couldn't he help me?

About a week later he came to my office to ask if he could borrow my car because he and a roommate were going on a double date. It's hard, he explained, for a girl to crawl into the backseat of a two-door car like his. Besides, my car was new and his was 10 years old. He wanted to make a good impression on the girls.

"No," I said, then responded to his shock: "It wasn't important to help me impress my visitor, but it is important for me to help you impress your date. Something's wrong here."

He stuck out his lower lip and I could see anger in his eyes. But the conversation ended there and I soon forgot about the exchange amidst my hectic day—until my secretary said, "Look out the window and you'll see repentance."

There, right under my office window—so I wouldn't miss it—my son was washing my car. I continued to work but from time to time I glanced down to see how he was doing. He opened wide the trunk and all the doors and meticulously swept the floorboards. Then he was gone for a while. I wondered where he had taken my car, and then he appeared in my office. He announced, "I even took it to the car wash to steam-clean the engine and get it waxed. Look and see." Together we stood at my window to admire the freshly waxed car shining in the afternoon sun.

"Ya like it?" he asked.

What could I say but yes?

"So, can I borrow it for that double date?"

"Yes!" I said gladly, knowing my son had learned an important lesson about repentance.

Even when we displease our heavenly Father, we are still His child. But just as an earthly father may withhold privileges from a stubborn son, so too our heavenly Father may withhold answers to our prayers until we repent—not out of spite, but in hopes that we will learn our lesson.

John tells us that God is faithful to forgive when we confess our sins (see 1 John 1:9). But confessing means more than admitting you did wrong. It means putting your repentance into action, like my son did that day. He was willing to please his earthly father by going the extra mile. He wanted to demonstrate his change of heart. I would have forgiven him anyway—just as the Father's forgiveness does not depend on our good works—but my son's actions showed his sincere repentance.

The Lord wants to give you good things—perhaps something even better than His car. But if you persist in unrepentance, He may withhold those blessings. Pray, "Forgive us our debts," today and then put your repentance into action.

Date Read: ______________________________

Scripture Reading: Luke 17:1-19

Memory Verse: "Let the words of my mouth and the meditation of my heart be acceptable in Your sight, O Lord, my strength and my Redeemer" (Ps. 19:14, *NKJV*).

Prayer Requests:______________________________

Lead Us Not into Temptation

Day 16

Don't Even Steal a Milky Way

I was about nine years old when I decided to steal from a local corner store. We didn't have a lot of money so I walked in the ditch on my way, looking for soda bottles. There was a two-cent deposit on each bottle, and three bottles were enough for a five-cent soda. Almost never did I find enough bottles for a candy bar to go with my soda.

I was browsing the store one day when my hand brushed over a box of Milky Way candy bars. Glancing up, I noticed the cashier didn't see me. In bed that night, I thought about picking up a Milky Way and walking out—stealing it.

The next day I "cased the joint" to see if I could do it. When the cashier wasn't looking, I picked up a Milky Way and hid it in my hand. Then I walked to the door. She didn't stop me, but I returned the Milky Way to its box—that had been my practice run. I planned to steal it for real the next day.

But the next day was Sunday and I was in the junior class at Eastern Heights Presbyterian Church. The teacher explained how Rachel had stolen her father's idols and hidden them in a saddlebag. He looked at us gravely and warned, "Don't ever steal anything—not even a Milky Way."

I was stunned! *Why did he say Milky Way? Who told him?* I mentally ran through a list of my friends' names, but then remembered I hadn't told anyone. That's when it hit me: *God told him.* Even a junior boy can be seized by conviction. That morning I realized God knew about my plans to steal a Milky Way. My heavenly Father spoke to me through that Sunday school teacher, and I didn't follow through with my plans for larceny—and I've been careful ever since not to take anything that doesn't belong to me!

One of the Ten Commandments is "Thou shalt not steal" (Exod. 20:15, *KJV*). Stealing hurts all parties involved, including God. Why is stealing so bad that God listed it between adultery and lying? Because stealing demonstrates that the thief's heart is committed to acquiring the stuff of this world, not to trusting the God from whom all blessings flow.

You will be presented with opportunities to steal. These opportunities are a test of your character—and when you resist the temptation, you strengthen your faith. James tells us to welcome such tests, "For you know that when your faith is tested, your endurance has a chance to grow. So let it grow, for when your endurance is fully developed, you will be perfect and complete, needing nothing" (Jas. 1:3-4). Remember, God may allow you to be tempted, but it is not God who tempts you. James continues: "God is never tempted to do wrong, and he never tempts anyone else. Temptation comes from our own desires, which entice us and drag us away" (Jas. 1:13-14, *NLT*).

What should you do when you are tempted? Realize there is a way to overcome or escape from temptation; God will not allow temptation to overpower you without offering you a way out. "No temptation has overtaken you except such as is common to man; but God is faithful, who will not allow you to be tempted beyond what you are able, but with the temptation will also make the way of escape, that you may be able to bear it" (1 Cor. 10:13, *NKJV*). Look for an exit! You overcome temptation when you walk away.

There is a victory available to those who struggle with temptation. Are you fasting and praying about a recurring temptation? Do you have an addiction so great that you have difficulty saying no?

Fasting will help you win victory. When you fast and pray, you're declaring that your needs and desires are not the primary thing in life. God is the focus of your life—and He is the source of your victory.

Date Read: ______________________________

Scripture Reading: 1 Corinthians 10:1-15

Memory Verse: "No temptation has overtaken you except such as is common to man; but God is faithful, who will not allow you to be tempted beyond what you are able, but with the temptation will also make the way of escape, that you may be able to bear it" (1 Cor. 10:13, *NKJV*).

Prayer Requests: ______________________________

Day 17

Whatcha Gonna Do If You Give Up?

You're just days away from the successful completion of your fast. So don't quit now! Don't even think about quitting. Remember the old adage: "Winners never quit, and quitters never win." What would you accomplish by quitting?

When I was 15 years old, I rode my bicycle from Savannah, Georgia, to my aunt Lelia's house in Orangeburg, South Carolina, a trip of about 120 miles. I began about 4:00 am. When the weather was cool, I could cover about 20 miles in one hour, followed by a short rest.

The sun got really hot around 11:00 am and there were no shade trees on the highway. As the day wore on, the summer sun got hotter and my enthusiasm waned. Now I could cover only 10 miles in one hour.

My body didn't want to give up; I was in good physical condition. It was my mind that slowed me down. I stopped at a country store for a cold drink and was tempted to stay in the shade. It was hard to convince myself to get back on the bicycle and launch out again.

When the sun was at its hottest, every bit of shade tempted me to stop and rest awhile. I daydreamed about giving up and phoning someone to come get me. But that was many years before cell phones and there were no pay phones in country stores. Besides, in those days long distance phone calls were expensive.

There were no motels where I could afford to sleep for the night and then finish tomorrow. I didn't know anyone who lived on the way to stay over at a friend's house. I even wondered if I could pretend to faint so an ambulance would come and take me to a hospital. At least there I could relax in an inviting bed. But I didn't feel like I was going to faint. I just felt discouraged.

I thought of every option, and there was not one way for me to quit.

So I rode on, miserable, feeling sorry for myself. But I kept peddling. My only option was to finish.

Around 4:00 pm I rode up to the front of Aunt Lelia's house. There was no brass bell to welcome me or crowds to cheer my victory. It was just Aunt Lelia. So I went into the kitchen for a glass of iced tea.

Standing in the kitchen, drinking that delicious tea, I realized there was something better than a cheering crowd. There was an inner pat on the back that was greater than any reward anyone could give me. I had done what I considered the unthinkable . . . the impossible . . . the incredible. I didn't know of any 15-year-old boys who had ridden that far in one day on a bicycle. And I had done it!

You are on the seventeenth day of a fast. Don't quit! If you give up now, you will be giving up 16 days of sacrifice. All those days of fasting would be wasted for just one bite. And you would be giving up your vow. Remember, you are fasting for a purpose. You began by writing out your prayer goal, then you signed your name. Let me ask you, is one bite of food worth it to give up the answer to prayer you are seeking from God?

You may feel desperate, as I did on that scorching highway, to find an option besides completing your goal. But when you look at all the options, the only one that makes sense is to finish. Intimacy with God and answers to prayer are far greater rewards than a full belly.

Date Read: ______________________

Scripture Reading: 2 Timothy 4:1-8

Memory Verse: "Therefore do not be ashamed of the testimony of our Lord, nor of me His prisoner, but share with me in the sufferings for the gospel according to the power of God" (2 Tim. 1:8, *NKJV*).

Prayer Requests: ______________________

Day 18

You Swam in Our Drinking Water

The temperature was way over a hundred degrees, and the Cuckoo Patrol was looking for someplace to cool off. David Mixon and Earl Fritz lived in houses on the property of Hillcrest Cemetery; both of their fathers worked as groundskeepers. High above David Mixon's house was the cemetery's water tank, which also supplied water to the five streets of our neighborhood, Wagner Heights. But the water tank didn't look like the towering cylindrical tanks you see in American small towns. Rather, the cemetery owners had built a high wooden platform, and on it they constructed a large wooden tank to hold water. It was about eight feet deep, and it looked more like a trough for horses than a water tower.

There was no roof on the tank and the cool water tempted the boys of the Cuckoo Patrol. We had climbed up to the platform before, but Mr. Mixon had always run us off. There were signs on all four posts that read "No Trespassing"—but that water looked so inviting!

No one was home at the Mixon or Fritz houses, so we thought no one would see us. We climbed up to the platform and stripped down to our birthday suits, crawling around army-style so no one from the neighborhood could see us. We scrambled up the sides of the tank and dove into the cool water. It was heaven.

But we let our guard down. Some of the guys climbed up on the side to dive in again and again. When you get away with something once, it's tempting to believe you can beat the odds.

After a good long swim, we laid on the platform to dry in the hot sun. Eventually we got dressed, sneaked down the back pole and went on our way.

When I got home that night, Mother said, "Mrs. Hoffman saw you swimming in the water tank." Then she added in quiet horror, "You swam in our drinking water."

Being only slightly wiser than the first time I lied, I answered, "I wasn't there; it was the other guys."

"Mrs. Hoffman specifically said she saw you up there."

I got a spanking for swimming in the neighborhood's water supply. I tried to rationalize with Mother—"The hot sun will kill all the germs!"—but it did no good. I also got a spanking for lying.

Why do we so often think we can walk right through the "No Trespassing" signs in this life? And why is our first reaction to lie when we are caught?

Many times, we think God's will is to keep us from having fun, when actually He is trying to keep us safe. There are consequences each time we rebel against God and break His law. Scripture says, "Do not be drunk with wine" (Eph. 5:18, *NKJV*), but not because God is a killjoy. He doesn't want us to get drunk and kill ourselves or someone else. Same with stealing, or lying, or sleeping with someone other than your spouse, or cheating, or hording our wealth, or making decisions by consulting a horoscope. God is trying to keep you safe and make you whole, not keep you from having fun.

Victory rarely comes in a last-minute deliverance when you are in the grips of temptation. Victory comes long before you are challenged to sin. The secret is deciding to be victorious long before entering a battle. The secret is in preparing to be victorious by learning God's Word, by walking in fellowship with Him, and in praying daily, "Lead us not into temptation."

Date Read: ________________________________

Scripture Reading: Luke 22:47-62

Memory Verse: "Therefore submit to God. Resist the devil and he will flee from you" (Jas. 4:7, *NKJV*).

Prayer Requests: ________________________________

____

____

____

____

____

____

____

____

____

____

____

____

Deliver Us from the Evil One

Day 19

Send Angels to Protect Him

When my wife, Ruth, was five years old, she prayed to receive Christ. Her mother, who led her in prayers every night, told her to begin praying for the man she would marry. So each evening Ruth prayed, "Lead my husband to be a Christian, make him strong and wise." Then she always added, "Send angels to protect him." And then she added a typical young girl's request: "Make him cute."

I grew up more than 1,000 miles away in Savannah, Georgia, but God answered that prayer of protection several times. One day I stepped on a snake and another time I fell out of a tree—neither caused any harm. I jumped on my bicycle when I was 15 years old and peddled to Orangeburg, South Carolina, 120 miles away. Who knows what could happen to a young teen boy on a highway miles from home? And I'm confident God protected me from dangers I won't ever know about this side of heaven. He may have sent guardian angels to watch over me. Jesus observed, "Beware that you don't look down on any of these little ones. For I tell you that in heaven their angels are always in the presence of my heavenly Father" (Matt. 18:10, *NLT*).

Each and every day, pray, "Deliver us from the Evil One." You don't know what dangers await you at the hands of the Adversary. The driver of a car heading toward you could be high on drugs. The food in a restaurant could be tainted with E-coli.

Once in Bombay, India, in an expensive revolving restaurant overlooking the Bay of Bengal, I thought the food would be safe. I had heard about the dangers of getting a bug and getting ill in India. *Okay,* I thought, *but a five-star hotel is different.*

"Don't drink the water," a fellow missionary warned me.

But I drank it. Actually, I drank bottled water, but I poured it over ice. Ten minutes later I fainted on the restaurant floor, and continued to pass out every two hours. It was only the help of God that got me back to the United States; I certainly didn't want to be stuck in a foreign hospital for an extended illness. As it turned out, I had that bug for almost an entire year before it passed completely from my system.

I travel often in various parts of the world, and I realized after that experience that there are many food traps the Evil One can use to thwart my ministry. One Saturday night I ate oyster stew, got food poisoning and threw up all night. I was sick until 30 minutes before I had to preach the following morning. I don't remember praying for God to protect me that day, but now "Deliver us from the Evil One" is a part of my prayer every morning.

Why must you pray for protection? Four reasons. First, this is a hostile world filled with snakes, hurricanes, poison weeds, germs and millions of other hazards, all results of the Fall (see Gen. 3). The earth feeds us, but it gives healthy enjoyable crops reluctantly. We have to cultivate the ground, plant, weed, water and protect our crops from fungi, insects, drought and storms. God can deliver and protect us from the hostilities of this fallen world.

Second, there are evil people in the world who mean us harm. They will steal from us, beat us up and attack us verbally and physically. God can deliver and protect us from evildoers.

Third, there is persistent evil in our hearts. We were born in sin (see Ps. 51:5) and evil has influenced every part of our life (see Rom. 3:10-23). We are blinded by our sinful nature and can convince ourselves we are doing the right thing even when we are harming ourselves (see Rom. 7:19). God can deliver and protect us from the evil in our own nature.

Finally, Satan hates God. Anyone on God's side is opposed by the Devil: "Be sober, be vigilant; because your adversary the devil walks about like a roaring lion, seeking whom he may devour" (1 Pet. 5:8, *NKJV*). When a lion is satisfied, he sits in his lair, but when he's hungry he walks about and roars. When you sense Satan is on the prowl for you, pray, "Deliver us from the Evil One."

Date Read: ________________________________

Scripture Reading: Exodus 13:21–14:31

Memory Verse: "No evil shall befall you, nor shall any plague come near your dwelling; for He shall give His angels charge over you, to keep you in all your ways" (Ps. 91:10-11, *NKJV*).

Prayer Requests: ________________________________

____

____

____

____

____

Day 20

Elmer, Don't Jump!

When I was a senior in high school I went with the youth department of Eastern Heights Presbyterian Church to a Friday night oyster roast in Thunderbolt, Georgia. The Wilmington River is a very large, deep river used by boats sailing the Intracoastal Waterway. The bridge over the Wilmington at Thunderbolt was a high drawbridge and the source of my temptation.

A bunch of us were drifting aimlessly in inner tubes while our chaperone followed in a rowboat. It was ebb tide (high tide) when I decided to show off. I bragged that I was going to climb to the top of the bridge and dive in. Betty Farthing, a fellow senior, began to yell, "Elmer, don't do it! You'll kill yourself!"

That kind of talk only eggs on a teenage boy, especially one who wants to show off for the girls. It was only when I got to the top of the bridge that I realized it was as tall as a three-story building. It was a long way down to the water. I knew the channel was deep and I wouldn't hit bottom, but I decided a head-first dive would kill me. It would have to be feet first.

As I prepared to make the leap, Betty was still screaming, "Elmer, don't do it! You'll kill yourself!"

But my ego was too strong. I couldn't crawl down the ladder; that humiliation would be worse than death, so I thought I might as well jump and kill myself. I almost jumped three or four times, but each time I thought better of it. My hesitation was my conscience trying to talk some sense into me. Suddenly, on an impulse, I threw myself over the side, yelling as loud as I could, "Yi-i-i-i-i-i-i-i-i . . . !"

I sounded like a Confederate lineman charging to his death under Yankee musket fire. I hit the water and went down . . . down . . . down. Then the greatest thought occurred to me: *I'm not dead.* Slowly I swam upward, and when I broke the surface, the cheers of the gang washed over me. Above them all I heard, "Oh, Elmer!" It was Betty's voice of adulation.

And that was all the glory I got that evening. Within just a few minutes, the gang was eating and talking about other things, and Betty Farthing went home with Charles Lomel later that evening.

A lot of the stupid things we do are not worth it.

When we pray, "Deliver us from the Evil One," we're not always praying against things "out there" like a car accident, or a tornado, or any other evil plan of Satan's to derail our life. Many times we are praying against our own inclinations to do stupid things. If I had dived headfirst, or hit the water at a wrong angle, I very well might have killed myself. Today, I thank God for looking after me when I was a stupid teenager and did stupid things just to show off to the girls.

But stupid isn't only showing off in physical feats of danger. Sometimes we need to pray, "Deliver us from the Evil One," to ask God to keep us from stupid financial schemes that would drive us into bankruptcy. We need to pray for God to keep us from doing stupid things that would cause us to lose our job, or put our children at risk, or even end us up in prison.

There's also another reason to pray, "Deliver us from the Evil One." Think of the many times in your life when you are not in control. What would happen if a child darts out in front of your car and was struck? Or if you were involved in an accident in which someone was maimed for life? You might not be responsible for what happened, but your vehicle destroyed another life. You may be asking God to deliver you from a lifetime of guilt, or from a financial penalty, or from a consequence that takes away your freedom.

One more thing I'd like to point out: I was with a church youth group, and none of them stopped me from doing something stupid. You can be on the Lord's business, even serving with Christians, but you still need to pray, "Deliver us from the Evil One."

Date Read: ______________________________

Scripture Reading: Matthew 4:1-11

Memory Verse: "Put on the whole armor of God, that you may be able to stand against the wiles of the devil" (Eph. 6:11, *NKJV*).

Prayer Requests: ______________________________

Day 21

I Couldn't Stop Cursing

Reggie McDuffy sat in front of me in the fourth grade. One day he turned to show me a curse word he had written on a sheet of paper. "Say it," he dared. My first response was, "No." I knew that one of the Ten Commandments was "You shall not take the name of the Lord your God in vain" (Exod. 20:7, *NKJV*). I was also pretty sure I would get a spanking if Mother heard me curse.

"Go ahead, say it." Reggie was quite the tempter.

I said the word inwardly, then I mouthed the word outwardly. Reggie laughed his approval.

Immediately I felt my fist get bigger. I sat taller in my seat. I felt manly. At recess, we played tag. A boy tagged me, pushing me down. I chased him relentlessly, pushing him down with a tag and cursing him. My legs were stronger and my muscles bulged under my shirt. I was no longer the puny kid in the class. I was now one of The Boys.

A few Sundays later I went to the Presbyterian youth meeting and saw a lit candle and metal bowl at the front of the room. It was Consecration Day. We were all given small pieces of paper on which to write our sins. They were to be placed in the metal bowl and set aflame with the candle. The fire was the symbolic purging of our sins. I wrote "cursing" on my paper. When it went up in flames, I figured I would quit cursing. But the next time a guy knocked me down at school, I cursed him. That began a cursing lifestyle. The only time I didn't curse was around my parents and other relatives. I couldn't control my cursing, even though I tried to stop—several times.

About a year later I went back to the Presbyterian youth meeting and again they had the flickering candle and metal bowl on the table up front. This time I "vowed" to clean up my mouth. I wrote down every curse word I could think of, even though I couldn't spell some of them. When the slips of paper were burnt up, I knew my cursing addiction was gone. But I was wrong. It came back in a moment of anger as if it had never left.

I continued to curse around my buddies, but not around women or family who might tell my mother. I knew she would spank me.

At the end of my junior year in high school I went back to the Presbyterian youth camp in Waycross, Georgia. The last night of camp there was a bonfire where several young people were giving testimonies. I jumped up to ask forgiveness for cursing. Throwing a wood chip into the fire, I promised never to curse again. I was convinced I was cured.

But a few weeks later I got my package of newspapers to deliver on my route. They were bound with wire. My practice was to bend the wire back and forth about 70 times until the wire broke, but this time it broke on the sixth or seventh bend and the ragged end ripped open my knuckle.

I cursed the wire.

"I thought you promised not to curse again," my friend Arthur Winn chided me.

"Oh, d--- you," I cursed him.

We were folding papers on the church porch because it was rainy. "Here comes the preacher," said Arthur, warning me to be quiet.

"Oh, d--- him," I cursed.

I didn't try to stop cursing for another year. On July 25, 1950, I was born again on a Thursday evening. I had joined the church at age 12 and professed salvation. Many times I had asked God to forgive my cursing, but it always came back.

But on a Thursday night after attending a revival meeting, I prayed by my bed around 11:15 to receive Christ. I surrendered completely to God. When I confessed my sins honestly, I felt the horrors of hell as though I was already there. I begged, "Jesus, come into my heart and save me." He did.

I jumped to my feet and pumped my fist in the dark bedroom. I knew I was saved because I had met a person: Jesus Christ.

I never cursed again. Not because of the Third Commandment; I had tried to keep the Law by legalism, but it hadn't worked. Trying to be good didn't work. Even empty promises, vows and self-discipline didn't keep me from cursing.

But now I had Jesus Christ in my heart. I had met the Son of God, who had transformed my life. It was His power that changed me. I rejoiced with the apostle Paul, "Christ lives in me; and the life which I now live in the flesh I live by faith in the Son of God, who loved me and gave Himself for me" (Gal. 2:20, *NKJV*).

When you pray "Deliver us from the Evil One," the secret of victory is not your ability to pray, or your ability to fast, or even your act of surrender. The secret is a person: Jesus Christ. The secret is the Powerful One: Jesus Christ. "If the Son makes you free, you shall be free indeed" (John 8:36, *NKJV*).

Perhaps you are fasting and praying for victory over an addiction. Fasting builds your self-discipline to give you spiritual strength, but taking hold of Christ's power is the only thing that will transform you. When you take control of the outward person by fasting, you begin to give Christ control of the inner person for victory. Surrender your inner person to the Savior, and allow His Spirit to transform you and lead you to victory.

Date Read: ______________________________

Scripture Reading: Matthew 17:1-23

Memory Verses: "And you shall know the truth, and the truth shall make you free. . . . Therefore if the Son makes you free, you shall be free indeed" (John 8:32,36, *NKJV*).

Prayer Requests:______________________________

____

____

____

____

____

____

____

____

____

____

____

____

____